WHAT ARE THEY
SALVATION?

What Are They Saying About Salvation?

Denis Edwards

PAULIST PRESS
New York/Mahwah

Library of Congress Cataloging-in-Publication Data

Edwards, Denis.
    What are they saying about salvation?

    Bibliography: p.
    1. Salvation—History of doctrines—20th century.
I. Title.
BT751.2.E34   1986   234   86-2425
ISBN 0-8091-2793-8 (pbk.)

Published by Paulist Press
997 Macarthur Boulevard
Mahwah, N.J. 07430

Printed and bound in the
United States of America

Contents

For

Archbishop James W. Gleeson

Preface

This volume grows out of reading and reflection done communally, through the Theology Institute of the church in Adelaide. I want to acknowledge the importance of the insights and the encouragement I have received from those who have participated in courses at the Theology Institute in the last two years.

On his retirement I dedicate this little book to Archbishop Gleeson of Adelaide, in thanksgiving for his pastoral leadership, particularly for the way in which he has supported the attempt to provide access to theology for the whole local church.

I am grateful to all those friends who have helped with this book, particularly Sr. Christine Burke, I.B.V.M., Sr. Barbara Agnew, C.PP.S., Marie Reitano and Genevieve Honner.

1
Salvation at the End
of the Twentieth Century

Most would agree that salvation is an absolutely central doctrine of Christian faith. However, there is no agreement about its meaning. Many of those who believe in salvation find it hard to say what they understand it to be. What is salvation? Is it something we actually experience? From what are we saved? For what are we set free?

A World in Need of Saving

The issue of salvation confronts us with unique urgency as we approach the end of the twentieth century. On the one hand we have a chance, unparalleled in history, to lift the burdens that weigh heavily on so many people. On the other hand we are face to face with evil on a scale that the human race has never before known. We stand at the brink of a hell of our own making.

The nuclear arms race is the most dangerous event in human history. At any moment a poor political decision, or even a mistake, can trigger a nuclear exchange that will extinguish all life on this planet. The precarious relationship between the super-powers puts our global future in doubt. This situation is made more perilous by the military expansion of smaller countries, the ease of access to nuclear technology, the development of "first-strike" policies, and the militarization of space. In this kind of world it is not surprising to find that even young children experience a disturbing anxiety about survival. Human consciousness is shaped today by a pervasive fear of global death.

If the threat of nuclear war is the most serious crisis facing the world, for millions of people the problems of hunger, malnutrition, unemployment and poverty are much more immediate. The resources spent on the arms race are stolen from the poor of the world. Huge companies, more powerful than many governments, exploit the poorer countries, draining them of wealth and maintaining their dependency. Within the richer countries the gap between the wealthy and the unemployed poor is widening. The economic and political exploitation of the poor of the world demands attention from anyone who would offer a theology of salvation today.

It is true that there has always been exploitation and we can rejoice that the human race has largely overcome certain specific forms of oppression like slavery and serfdom. But the earth has never known poverty on the scale we have today. In the same way we human beings have always used up finite resources, but we have never before had to face the fact that our consumption threatens the future of the planet. The combination of a staggering population growth in this century, and the cynical exploitation of the environment for economic gain, has meant the irreversible loss of much of the earth's bounty. Only urgent and communal action offers us any hope for the survival of the earth's resources, and it is only by "befriending" the earth that we can hope for human survival.

The arms race, the exploitation and misery of the poor, and the rapid depletion of the earth's resources constitute a threefold crisis that offers humanity at the end of this century a simple choice between life and death. A Christian theology of salvation must find the capacity to speak to this crisis.

There is a fourth issue of our time which is a sign of hope. Throughout the world women are beginning to become aware of the way in which they have been held in a position of inferiority through the long history of patriarchal society. They are beginning to participate in a movement aimed at equality and the sharing of power. It is becoming clear that this movement constitutes the start of a massive shift in human consciousness that will have far-reaching effects in our history. Perhaps it will be only through the emergence of women, and the release of the potential of half the human race, that we will be able to deal with the crisis formed by nuclear confrontation, economic exploitation of the poor and ecological irresponsibility.

I believe that these four issues constitute the unique context in which Christians today must ask about God's salvation. Of course there are other urgent questions which I cannot deal with here, but I want simply to argue that a contemporary theology of salvation must have something to say about these four issues, and must offer some grounds for hope and a basis for action. Some of the questions that emerge from these reflections are these: Does salvation from God concern only personal liberation from sin, or does it concern also liberation from war, exploitation, environmental pollution and the domination of women? If God's salvation does have to do with these issues as well as sin and guilt, how does it take effect in our history? Are we to see salvation as happening through our own liberating activity—through, for example, participation in the peace movement, or the sharing of action and reflection in a basic Christian community?

There are further questions that emerge about salvation today. We are conscious of the long history of humanity that preceded the life of Jesus of Nazareth, of the millions alive today and throughout history who have never heard the Gospel, and of those who have rejected a distorted or mistaken view of the Gospel. How is the God of Jesus Christ engaged with all these people? How do we account for their salvation? If Christians believe that salvation comes through faith in Jesus Christ, how can those be saved who have not known him? There is the strong Christian conviction that Christ died "for us," that in some mysterious way his life, death and resurrection are the cause of our salvation. How can Jesus' death be the cause of salvation if God was already at work offering salvation to all women and men?

A further series of questions emerge from theology's recovery of Jesus' view of God. If God is a God of boundless compassion, a God who is Abba, then this raises difficulties with some traditional Christian understandings of the redemption. When, for example, the death of Jesus is understood as the price paid in order to placate the wrath of God, then this view of redemption seems in conflict with a Christian theology of God. But if the cross of Jesus is not about placating God, how is it related to our salvation? How is it the cause of our redemption?

Before turning to some contemporary theologians to see how they answer these questions, it will be helpful to look briefly at some of the theologies of salvation that we find in the New Testament and in Christian tradition.

Salvation in the New Testament

There is a sense in which the whole of the New Testament is concerned with salvation. Each book deals with the transformation of human existence through the life, death and resurrection of Jesus. In the brief space available here I will consider only five of the concepts by which the New Testament expresses the meaning of Jesus for us: redemption, expiation, justification, liberation and salvation.

Redemption

The English word redemption translates the Greek word *apolytrōsis,* which means a buying back or a ransom (*lytron*). In Mark's Gospel Jesus is seen as the Son of Man who "came not to be served but to serve, and to give his life as a ransom for many" (10:45). In the infancy stories of Luke Zechariah praises God, "for he has visited and redeemed his people" (1:68), and Anna is found speaking of Jesus "to all who were looking for the redemption of Jerusalem" (2:38). Paul sees our redemption as "in Christ Jesus" (Romans 3:24) and he sees Jesus as the one whom God has made our redemption (1 Corinthians 1:30). In a related image Paul writes: "You were bought with a price" (1 Corinthians 6:20; 7:23). Those who were under the law have been redeemed from the law and become adopted children (Galatians 3:13; 4:5). In the letter to Titus Jesus is seen as the one "who gave himself up for us to redeem us from all iniquity and to purify for himself a people of his own who are zealous for good deeds" (2:14).

The image of "buying back" has its roots in Hebrew family law where the *go'el* was the close relative whose duty it was to buy back goods and persons that had become someone else's property. There was also the law of the marketplace where one could buy back (*pâdâ*) the life of a slave. In the Hebrew Scriptures God is the Redeemer of the people, the One who pays the ransom price for the people: "I am the Lord, and I will bring you out from under the burdens of the Egyptians, and I will deliver you from their bondage and I will redeem you with an outstretched arm and with great acts of judgment, and I will take you for my people, and I will be your God" (Exodus 6:6–7). The most important source for the image of redemption in the New Testament is the Jewish people's experience of both their deliverance from Egypt and their union with God through the Sinai covenant.

God's redemption of us through the death and resurrection of

Jesus is a movement of deliverance from sin and evil and a movement of communion with the living God. When the word "redemption" is used to describe this, then clearly we have a metaphor at work. God's saving action is being described as a "buying back." The emphasis in the metaphor is on the helpless situation of those ransomed, and on the liberating activity of God. If the metaphor is pushed too far it is possible to ask who receives payment, but this is not the direction of biblical thought. In the Scriptures no one claims or receives a price in the exodus, and no one claims or receives a price in the death and resurrection of Jesus. The death of Jesus is not a price paid to Satan and it is certainly not a price paid by humanity to God. It is God who acts to redeem humanity through the life, death and resurrection of Jesus.

Expiation

The Greek word *hilaskomai* (with the noun *hilasmos*) can be translated in English as either "to expiate" (sins) or "to propitiate" (God). The word is not used often in the New Testament. In Paul we find a single reference:[1] "They are justified by his grace as a gift, through the redemption which is in Christ Jesus, whom God put forward as an expiation by his blood, to be received by faith" (Romans 3:24). The image of expiation is found in 1 John (2:2; 4:10) and in Hebrews where the author argues that Jesus "had to be made like his brethren in every respect, so that he might become a merciful and faithful high priest in the service of God, to make expiation for the sins of the people" (2:17).

There is an important Jewish feast, described in Chapter 16 of Leviticus, called the Day of Atonement. The Hebrew word is *kippèr* which means to "cover over," or to atone for sins through a peace offering. The basic thought is that of rendering a person pleasing to God. However, in Jewish thought it is always God who forgives. The community may dispose itself to receive the gift of God but it is God who takes away sin. In normal Greek usage the word *hilaskomai* could have as its object a divine being. Human persons propitiate a god. However in the New Testament it is God who expiates our sins, and thus manifests good will and makes peace: "In this is love, not that we loved God but that he loved us and sent his Son to be the expiation for our sins" (1 John 4:10).

The New Testament, then, does not have a theology of placating or propitiating God. It does have a theology of the expiation of sins, but it is God who expiates. In the priestly sacrifice of ancient Israel the expiation was performed by a priest, but it was clearly recognized that only God could forgive. When the New Testament understands Jesus' death against the background of the Jewish theology of atoning sacrifice, then Jesus' death can be called an expiation. But this expiation has its source in God. Expiation and forgiveness occur as one act of God in the death and resurrection of Jesus.

Justification

For Paul the whole action of God in Christ Jesus can be discussed in the language of justification or righteousness (*dikaiosynē*). Paul's understanding of righteousness is found in compact form in Romans 3:21–26:

> But now the righteousness of God has been manifested apart from the law, although the law and the prophets bear witness to it, the righteousness of God through faith in Jesus Christ for all who believe. For there is no distinction; since all have sinned and fall short of the glory of God, they are justified by his grace as a gift, through the redemption which is in Christ Jesus, whom God put forward as an expiation by his blood, to be received by faith. This was to show God's righteousness, because in his divine forbearance he had passed over former sins; it was to prove at the present time that he himself is righteous and that he justifies him who has faith in Jesus.

Here many of Paul's major themes emerge. Justice or righteousness is first of all an attribute of God. It is not something we can earn through performance. It is something that comes to us as grace, as free gift. The requirement of the person justified is faith in Christ Jesus. Paul is arguing that the law is no longer the principle of salvation. Christ is the only way of salvation. In verse 24 Paul piles up images for Christ's saving action: he is our justification, grace, redemption, expiation. In those justified through faith in Jesus good works are the expression and consequence of God's justifying grace. God's righteousness, God's justice, expresses itself in mercy. Guilty men and women are declared and constituted as righteous by the free gift of a righteous and merciful God.

The image behind the concept of righteousness is that of just and proper relationships between people. It is the language of law. However, the Greek word *dikaiosynē* takes over the richness of the Hebrew *ṣᵉdâqâ*. This word described the attitude which sustains a covenant between two parties. In ancient Israel it referred to a social situation of peace and well-being, of right relations with all, which is the fruit of a good life before God.

If *ṣᵉdâqâ* always has a sense of being judged right by others, the believing person recognized that being right in God's eyes is the only thing that really matters. Being right before God is the profoundly religious understanding of righteousness that Paul inherits from his Jewish tradition. It is God who makes us righteous, through the free gift of love lavished on us in the death and resurrection of Jesus.

Liberation

The verb *eleutheroō* describes the action by which people are liberated from slavery. Paul, particularly, describes the event of salvation as a liberation. He is unrelenting in his defense of Christian freedom: "For freedom Christ has set us free; stand fast, therefore, and do not submit again to a yoke of slavery" (Galatians 5:1). Christ has liberated us from bondage to the law (Galatians 5:1–12), from sin (Romans 6:14–23) and from death (1 Corinthians 15). The liberating work of Christ cannot be restricted to individual life. It has cosmic dimensions since "creation itself will be set free from its bondage to decay and obtain the glorious liberty of the children of God" (Romans 8:21).

As the great liberation of the exodus freed the Hebrew people from slavery that they might be covenanted to God, so the freedom won in the death and resurrection of Jesus is no freedom for licentious conduct (Galatians 5:13; 2 Peter 2:19), but it is freedom for life in Christ. The biblical notion of freedom is freedom from certain realities, like sin, death, the law, anxiety, the fear of demons, hopelessness, a self-centered life, materialism, the need for prestige and power. However, just as important is the fact that it is freedom for such things as a life of discipleship, joy, commitment to truth and justice, loving relationships, making peace, sharing in the new creation of all things in Christ, hospitality, the sharing of goods, prayer and worship.

The Synoptic Gospels describe Jesus as one who went about freeing people through his healing, his exorcisms, his acts of forgiveness, and his relationships with them. Above all he preached and lived out a liberating view of God and the kingdom. In John's Gospel the life that comes from a disciple's relationship with the Lord is described as freedom: "If you continue in my word, you are truly my disciples, and you will know the truth, and the truth will make you free" (8:31); "So if the Son makes you free, you will be free indeed" (8:36).

In Luke's Gospel we find the ministry of Jesus encapsulated in what he reads to the congregation in the synagogue in Nazareth (in this text the word is *aphesis,* meaning release, rather than *eleutheria*): "The Spirit of the Lord is upon me, because he has anointed me to preach good news to the poor. He has sent me to proclaim release to the captives and recovering of sight to the blind, to set at liberty those who are oppressed, to proclaim the acceptable year of the Lord." (Luke 4:18–19)

Salvation

The New Testament can often express what God does in Jesus as salvation (*sōtēria*, with the verb *sōzō*). The Greek word has the meanings of being snatched away from peril, of being healed, of being preserved in health and well-being. From the Hebrew Scriptures it translates *yāšīᶜ*, which means to help in time of distress, and *pālat*, which means to rescue or deliver.

Paul uses the word only to describe the relationships between humanity and God. Salvation, for Paul, has a future, eschatological reference. It has the sense of escaping the wrath of the day of judgment and sharing in bodily resurrection (Romans 5:9; 10:9; 1 Corinthians 3:15; 5:5). For Paul salvation means sharing in the divine glory and being conformed to the image of the Son (Romans 8:29–30).

In the Synoptic Gospels the word occurs eighteen times in stories of healing by Jesus. Very often it occurs in the phrase "Your faith has made you well (saved you)" (Mark 5:34; 10:52; Luke 7:50; 17:19). In Mark we find the summary statement "And wherever he came, in villages, cities or country, they laid the sick in the marketplaces, and besought him that they might touch even the fringe of his garments; and as many as touched it were made well (saved)" (6:56). Jesus saves when he heals the sick, forgives sin, and rescues Peter and the disciples in a storm (Matthew 8:25; 14:30). In Luke's Gospel Jesus responds to Zacchaeus: "Today salvation has come to this house, since he also is a son of Abraham. For the Son of man came to seek and save the lost" (19:9–10). In the infancy stories Matthew comments on the name Jesus, which means "Yahweh saves" (1:21), and Luke has Mary rejoice in God her Savior (1:47), Zechariah bless God for the coming of salvation (1:69, 71, 77), the angels announce the birth of "a Savior, who is Christ the Lord" (2:11), and Simeon hold the infant in his arms and declare that his eyes have seen God's salvation (2:30).

The word Savior, although not frequent in the New Testament, is often found in the pastoral Epistles and in 2 Peter. It is used six times of God and four times of Christ in the pastorals. God is presented as the bringer of universal salvation, the one "who desires all men to be saved" (1 Timothy 2:4). When Jesus is called "Savior" (Titus 1:4; 2:13; 3:6; 2 Timothy 1:10) in the late New Testament period there seems to be an implication that Jesus, not the emperor, is truly the Savior, the benefactor who brings real salvation to the whole world. In 2 Peter the word Savior is used only of Jesus (1:1, 11; 2:20; 3:2, 18).

Even a brief consideration of these five words—redemption, expiation, justification, liberation and salvation—shows that each of them is a metaphor with resonances from everyday life as well as from the long Jewish religious tradition. The early Church struggled to express God's action in Jesus Christ by appealing to all kinds of human experience: buying back the lost or enslaved, the temple experience of atonement, establishing proper and legal relationships, freedom from slavery, and being snatched away from peril and given health and well-being.

I have been able to consider only a handful of the New Testament images which attempt to express the mystery of salvation. I believe it is important to recognize that each is a human and limited concept which attempts to express what finally escapes adequate expression. The very diversity of the New Testament theologies of salvation, and metaphors for salvation, both speaks of the vitality of the early Church's experience of God's saving action, and also makes clear that for the New Testament Church no one image or theology was absolute.

Traditional Theologies of Salvation

When a twentieth century Christian looks back over two thousand years of Christian experience it is hard to escape the conclusion that we have not done very well in our attempts to rethink the theology of salvation. There are, of course, the highly significant theologies of Augustine, Aquinas and Luther. But when one looks for a new vision, for creative metaphors, for original theology, then the list is quite short. I will mention only three approaches that are important, either positively or negatively, for our contemporary understanding of salvation.

Recapitulation

St. Irenaeus (c. 135–c. 202) had a cosmic view of salvation. He saw the whole of history as one great drama with three acts: first there was God's original creation; then there was human sin and the reign of evil; finally there is the restoration of the world to what God had intended through the life, death and resurrection of Jesus Christ. The work of redemption is seen as God's victory over the power of evil. Humankind is gathered together under the new Adam, Jesus Christ. God overcomes divisions caused by sin; now spirit and flesh, Jew and Gentile, are made one.[2] Irenaeus' key word for this process is "recapitulation" (Ephesians 1:10). The work of redemption is the restoration of all things under the headship of Christ:

> For we have shown that the Son of God did not begin to exist then since he always existed with the Father. But when he became incarnate and was made man, he recapitulated in himself the long line of the human race, procuring for us salvation summarily, so that what we had lost in Adam, that is, being in the image and likeness of God, we should regain in Jesus Christ.[3]

Christ saves our flesh by being united to us in the flesh. He passed through various stages of life, so that each stage might be sanctified.[4] Because we are recapitulated in Christ we are once again in God's image and likeness, we once more share God's life as adopted children, and we are destined for immortality and eternal communion with God. Jesus died on the cross that he might be "first-born from the dead, that in everything he might be pre-eminent" (Colossians 1:18).[5] He was raised in the flesh so that we might be raised with him. All of human life, all of creation, is recapitulated in Jesus Christ.

Deification

St. Athanasius (c. 295–373) is one of the strongest advocates of the view that we become deified in and through Christ (*Theopoiesis*). Toward the end of his *De Incarnatione* we find a sentence that is often quoted: "For he was made man that we might be made God."[6]

Against the Arians Athanasius strongly defended the Nicene doctrine of the divinity of Christ. He argued that the Logos must be God, since the re-creation of true humanity could only be accomplished by God. Athanasius understands salvation as re-creation and deification. Humankind would have lived "as God" if it had not been for the fall. The Logos now takes on humanity so that we may be renewed and deified. For Athanasius deification is very close to the biblical concept of becoming a son or daughter of God.[7] We never become gods in the way that the Logos is God and Son of God. He is Son by nature; we are sons and daughters of God by grace. Arius appeared to believe that the Logos was son in the same way we are. Athanasius insists that the Logos is God and true Son by nature. Unless this is so there is no adoption and we are not deified.[8] Christ had to share the divinity of the Creator and the humanity of the creature in order that humankind might be enabled to participate in God.

Deification has remained an evocative way of understanding God's action in Jesus Christ among Orthodox Christians. It has also had a long history in the Catholic tradition, where it has been used by the great mystical writers to express the transforming action of God upon the human soul.[9]

Satisfaction

During the Patristic era there were those who took the redemption image in a too literal fashion. They ended up believing that the death of Jesus was a price paid for our salvation either to God or to the devil. St. Anselm of Canterbury (1033–1109) in his book on the redemption *Cur Deus Homo?* worked out his own theory of satisfaction in such a way that it avoided the excesses of these earlier views.

Anselm's theory is built around an understanding of justice and proper relationship between God and humankind. Sin injures this proper relationship because it is a massive insult to God's honor. Because God is just and honorable this terrible distortion cannot be ignored. How is justice to be restored?

Only one who is divine can offer satisfaction for an insult against the infinite God; only one who is human can offer satisfaction for the sins of human persons.[10] Satisfaction can be offered, then, only by one who is God incarnate. Christ, by his obedience even to the point of death, offered a fully adequate, vicarious satisfaction for the infinite offense of human sin. Through God's action in the life, death and resurrection of Jesus, justice and right relationships are restored.

This theory of Anselm has much to recommend it, and it has been extraordinarily influential in subsequent theology. It avoids presenting God as one who cruelly demands reparation. Anselm does manage to show that God's act in the redemption is an act of love and generosity toward humanity. God restores right relationships out of love. In the process, however, Anselm's theory tends to suggest that God could only act within the framework of medieval notions of right order and right relationship.[11] Anselm's approach, perhaps, does not allow God the sovereign freedom to shatter human expectations by an act of unthinkable mercy.

Anselm's satisfaction theory has little appeal for most people today, perhaps because we do not share Anselm's medieval world view. However the biggest problem with this view of the redemption is that in popular preaching and teaching the satisfaction theory has been misunderstood and distorted. Instead of Anselm's careful thought we are presented with a vision of a God who demands satisfaction for offenses committed, like some powerful lord who is placated only by suffering and blood. In this distorted form the satisfaction theory has done immense harm.

Salvation has always been a central concern of Protestant theology, and writers like Barth, Brunner, Tillich, Pannenberg and Moltmann have made major contributions to our understanding of God's saving grace. Recently, however, Catholic theologians have shown new interest in the great question of salvation, and it is this new interest I am attempting to outline in this book. In the pages that follow I will discuss the positions of Karl Rahner, Gustavo Gutierrez, Sebastian Moore, and Edward Schillebeeckx. In approaching each of them I will have in mind the questions raised in this opening chapter.

2
Karl Rahner

Salvation as Co-Extensive with World History

More than any other theologian of our time Karl Rahner has struggled with the question whether God's salvation is available only through explicit faith in Jesus Christ or whether it is available to all men and women. Countless millions of people throughout history, before and since Jesus of Nazareth lived in Galilee two thousand years ago, have never had the Christian Gospel preached to them. Others have rejected inadequate presentations of Christian faith. Are all of these people able to share in salvation?

Rahner answers this question with a clear yes. He accepts the traditional doctrine that salvation is given us in the life, death and resurrection of Jesus, and he accepts that each person is saved through a free act of faith. However, he argues, it is not necessary that this be an explicit act of faith in the Good News of Jesus Christ. Someone who has never heard of the Gospel may be saved through an implicit faith.

In order to understand Rahner's theology on this issue it is helpful to follow his thought through three stages. The first stage is his anthropology.[1] He sees the human person as someone who lives in a world of incomprehensible mystery. Whenever a person uses the intellect to think about and grasp a specific reality (like another person, a tree, or the argument of a book), then the specific thing is grasped along with, or over against, an implicit awareness of the whole range of being that is without limits. We know specific objects against an horizon of infinite mystery. When we know anything there is already a question about infinity arising, perhaps only implicitly, at the edge of our consciousness. When we love, too, we can find that our love for another person is mysterious in its origin, and mysterious in that it seems to transcend the two persons and reach out to embrace all that is. In our knowing and loving we are confronted with the transcendence of the human person. There is something which is essential to us, which is at the core of our knowing and loving, which we cannot account for. To be human is to have an orientation toward the infinite, toward what is incomprehensible mystery.

Christian revelation adds the second all-important stage to the argument. Through revelation we know that God is not distant and removed, but always turning toward us offering love and forgiveness. The Christian Gospel reveals that God's love is offered to us in a free and forgiving self-communication. God is present in intimacy and closeness, always offering grace to the human person through the outpouring of the Holy Spirit. What God gives is nothing other than God's self. Creatures, while remaining creatures, can participate in God's being and can be called sons and daughters of God. God, without losing independence of being, is given to creatures as their own fulfillment.[2]

Human experience, then, reveals that a person is always confronted with transcendence and mystery. Christian revelation reveals that this transcendence and mystery is nothing else than the experience of God's self-communication in grace. The human person, according to Karl Rahner, is "the event of a free, unmerited and forgiving, and absolute self-communication of God."[3]

This means that all men and women stand under the offer of grace. This offer is permanent and ever-present. It always determines human existence. This state of affairs is what Karl Rahner calls the "supernatural existential."[4] Here we are at the third stage of Rahner's argument. Rahner wants to argue that God's presence and self-offering constitutes a permanent modification of the human spirit. Yet this always-present offer is not something due to human beings. It is always experienced as supernatural, as sheer gift. According to Rahner we are never in a "natural" (as opposed to a "supernatural") state. Because of God's free decision we find ourselves always in a supernatural world, a world determined by God's constant self-offering. The concept of "nature" is helpful, even though in the concrete we never find ourselves in a situation of pure nature, but always in a grace-determined existence. When we become aware of the fact that our supernatural existence is not owed to us, but a free gift, then we can mentally subtract this gift from our life and understand what nature means.[5]

This always-present self-offering of God is not something we experience as one object amongst other objects of experience. Rather it is experienced only implicitly in moments of mystery and transcendence in life. Christian believers can know that in the mystery there is the presence of a God of intimacy and love, and they can respond to this holy mystery in explicit faith.

God's self-offering to the whole of humankind is, by definition, salvation.[6] However, it is by no means an automatic salvation of an individual. God's offer of self-communication is made always and everywhere to each person, but an individual may accept or reject the offer that is made. When God's self-offering is accepted in freedom, then salvation takes hold in the person through justifying grace. A person may choose to reject the offer that is made and freely embrace sin. Sinful rejection of God's self-communication is always possible for a free person.

Rahner can say that "anyone who does not close himself to God in an ultimate act of his life and his freedom through free and personal sin for which he is really and subjectively guilty and for which he cannot shirk responsibility, this person finds his salvation."[7] A person may respond to God's self-offering with a clear and explicit faith, a faith whose content has been formed by long exposure to the Christian Gospel. But what about the non-believer, the person who has never heard the Gospel preached or the atheist who has considered Christianity but not been able to accept it? Can such people be saved? Rahner would say yes to this question.[8] A non-believer lives his or her life before the constant offer of God's self-communication. This reality is part of a person's existential constitution as a human being, because of God's free gift. Non-believers may say yes to this gift when they accept themselves completely, when they freely act according to conscience, when they live an ordinary day with love and care for others. According to Rahner this kind of acceptance is an implicit form of faith and it is rightly understood as supernatural faith. A person saying yes to conscience is also saying yes to the profound mystery that lies at the heart of human existence.

It is quite possible, then, for a non-believer to be freely saying yes to God's self-communication in an implicit way even though the person concerned might think and say that he or she does not believe in God or in Jesus Christ. A Marxist woman might reject Christian faith as an opiate, yet in her faithful commitment to the poor of history, Rahner would discern a fundamental yes to the mystery at the heart of life. A tribal man may never have come across the Gospel in any meaningful way, but in his love and respect for his traditional ritual, Rahner would see an implicit and salvific faith.

Rahner has described this situation as that of the "anonymous Christian." It is possible for a person to have an implicit saving faith and yet not be a Christian at the level of explicit concepts and language. The concept of the "anonymous Christian" has been criticized for various reasons. Some think it removes the motivation for missionary work. This objection ignores the fact that Rahner would argue that implicit faith, while it is salvific, still needs to reach its goal which is explicit faith in the liberating good news of Jesus Christ. Others say that the language ''anonymous Christian'' is self-contradictory, others still that it is a patronizing expression to use of those who freely choose not to be Christians. It is important to remember, in connection with this last point, that this theology is meant to help *Christians* account for the salvation of others from within their own framework.

While the terminology may be open to criticism,[9] I think that Rahner's basic theological position is well justified. He has argued for a massive shift in Christian thinking from a pessimistic stance with regard to salvation of those outside the Church (''outside the Church no salvation''). Rahner can look with satisfaction at the documents of Vatican II, where it is clearly and unambiguously taught that God's saving grace is not limited to the confines of the visible Church, but reaches out to all men and women.[10] If it is true that both pessimistic and optimistic views of the extent of salvation have existed side by side in Christian theological history, with Vatican II the optimistic view has become clearly a matter of Catholic doctrine.

For Karl Rahner, then, salvation is always both transcendental and historical at the same time. It is transcendental because it is always concerned with God's self-communication and human acceptance or rejection of this, and this exchange can never be recaptured completely in reflection. It is always historical because transcendence occurs in and through historical events, and our response to God's self-communication finds expression in our concrete encounters with day to day life.

This means that wherever human history is lived, there the history of salvation or its rejection takes place. Salvation does not necessarily have to be mediated by religious words or cults, but takes place in and through ordinary history. However, the experience of transcendence, and saving grace, does find expression in the religious language and customs of people who are not Christians. This means, Rahner believes, that we can suppose that there are supernatural, grace-filled, revelatory elements in non-Christian religions. He accepts that Christianity understands itself as an absolute religion finally intended for all. He also accepts that there may be human distortions and evil in different religions. But we are entitled to believe that for an individual in a pre-Christian situation, a non-Christian religion can be a means of salvation, included in God's plan of salvation.[11]

God is experienced at the heart of human existence in the world, but experienced as mystery. In the light of Christian revelation we know that this mystery is the place where we meet the always-present saving self-communication of God. We respond to this grace in the way we live our lives. This response may be an initial implicit faith, a faith which is itself justifying as long as the human response is faithful and honest. This is true for non-believers as well as for those able to make an explicit act of faith. Our very response is a gift of God. This is the structure of salvation according to Karl Rahner.

Jesus Christ, Sacrament of Salvation

If human salvation is understood as God's self-communication by grace to a person, and if this means that salvation is universally possible because of God's presence, at least as offer, to all conscious and free persons, then this raises an important theological question. How is salvation related to Jesus Christ? In Rahner's view men and women who lived before Jesus, and non-believers who have lived since, are not excluded from the possibility of salvation. Yet the New Testament and a constant Christian tradition say that we are saved by Jesus Christ, more particularly by his death and resurrection. How can the death and resurrection of Jesus be considered the cause of our salvation, if salvation is universally available? How can Jesus be a cause of salvation for people who lived thousands of years before him?

Rahner rejects a theology which would say only that Jesus'

death has exemplary significance for us. Although Jesus' death does show us how to open ourselves out in trust to God, Christian tradition insists that there is more to it than this. The tradition asserts that Jesus died "for us," that his death means something for our salvation, that in some way it is the cause of our salvation. How is this central conviction of faith to be explained in the light of Rahner's view of salvation as God's self-communication?

Another way of posing the question emerges from a consideration of the distinction in Rahner's thought between "self-redemption" and objective redemption.[12] By self-redemption Rahner means that we human beings can freely respond to God's self-offering, and in this sense redeem ourselves. Of course our very capacity to accept God's self-communication is itself a gift of God. There is no redemption, and no human fulfillment, apart from God's grace. But we can speak of self-redemption legitimately since salvation occurs in us through a fully human free act which is also always an event of grace. "Objective redemption" is a traditional term which refers to the death and resurrection of Jesus as cause of our salvation. The basic question then is how our "self-redemption" is related to "objective redemption."

The question about how the cross is the cause of our salvation becomes more acute when we rule out a common explanation: that the death of Jesus propitiates the wrath of God. In this view the death of Jesus causes God to change. Rahner completely rejects this view for three reasons. First, it wrongly assumes that God's mind and will can be changed. Second, it forgets that the initiative in salvation comes from God alone. Finally, it forgets that salvation can only take place through God's self-communication being accepted in human freedom. It is not that the cross causes God to will our salvation. Rather we must say that because God wills our salvation Jesus lived among us, died for us and is risen from the dead. Rahner writes: "God is not transformed from a God of anger and justice into a God of mercy and love by the cross; rather God brings the event of the cross to pass since he is possessed from the beginning of gratuitous mercy and, despite the world's sin, shares himself with the world, so overcoming its sin.''[13] Traditional ideas, like explaining the death of Jesus as an expiatory sacrifice, or like the theory of satisfaction of St. Anselm of Canterbury, have their own value but they become unhelpful when they are pushed too far. Then they run the terrible risk of distorting who God is. Then there is a grave danger of forgetting that the cross is not to be attributed to a vengeful God demanding recompense, but that its origin is in the mercy and love of a God who wants our salvation.

An answer to the question of how the death and resurrection of Jesus is related to our salvation must, then, take account of the following factors: (1) it must account for the availability of salvation for all men and women; (2) it must show a real causal connection between Jesus' death and our salvation, rather than simply a connection by way of example or by way of the moral impact which that death has upon us; (3) it must not distort God into an angry Lord demanding vengeance but it must make clear that the death and resurrection of Jesus are the expression of a God of boundless mercy and eternal love.

Rahner asks himself how Jesus thought of his own death. He answers that we can know, as a bare minimum, that Jesus accepted his death freely, surrendering himself to the ''unforeseen and incalculable possibilities of his existence.'' We can also know that in his death Jesus maintains ''his unique claim to an identity between his message and person in the hope that in his death he will be vindicated by God with regard to his claim.''[14] Jesus had preached the saving nearness of God, and he had claimed that this reign of God was identified with his own person. This claim is entrusted to God in the death of Jesus. With the resurrection experience the claim made by Jesus is given permanent validity and is shown to be vindicated by God. The resurrection shows that Jesus is indeed the final and unsurpassable self-disclosure of God. He is the absolute Savior.

The experience of the crucified and risen Jesus as absolute Savior is translated by New Testament writers into categories like "sacrifice" and "ransom." Rahner regards these as legitimate but secondary attempts to explain the meaning of Christ's death for our salvation.[15] Of themselves they do not offer an adequate answer for today to the question about the relationship between the death of Jesus and human salvation.

Rahner's basic thesis is that the death and resurrection are connected to the salvation of all men and women by way of sacramental causality.[16] He takes over a concept which is familiar in sacramental theology and uses it to illuminate the theology of salvation. The cross is a sacramental cause of our salvation in that it is the sign and the mediation of God's salvation. It is the sign of the "victorious and irreversible" saving activity of God in our world.

Not all signs actually cause what they signify. But a truly sacramental sign does cause the grace that is symbolized. Rahner believes that a sacrament is what he calls a "real symbol," an historical and social embodiment of grace. Grace achieves irreversible historical expression through the real symbol which is the sacramental sign. This means that grace and the sign of grace are mutually inter-related. There is a sense in which a sacramental sign is caused by grace, and there is a sense in which it embodies and expresses grace and can truly be said to cause grace.

Of course this concept cannot be arbitrarily used to explain the meaning of the death of Jesus. Our understanding of the cross and resurrection must come from a study of these events. However Rahner argues that when we look closely at Jesus' life, death and resurrection in the context of the history of salvation then the concept of the cross as a sacramental cause of salvation makes sense.

In order to see the force of this argument it is necessary to consider the whole history of salvation as one history in which God is present as offer to all human persons, a human solidarity in salvation which embraces all of history. Yet this universal experience of God's self-communication is always mysterious and indefinable. It is not explicit and concrete. There is always something ambivalent about this history of God's self-communication and our free response to God.

In this situation God could choose to give concrete and irreversible expression in history to divine saving love. God could choose to give fixed historical form to the universal will to save. This would be the case if God's self-communication to an individual were to occur in such a way that this one person became the irreversible self-giving of God to the world. This individual free person might also freely accept God's gift of self. This free acceptance would operate in all the person's actions and culminate in the acceptance of death. This is Rahner's understanding of what happens in the history of Jesus of Nazareth.[17] In this individual God's salvific will established itself irrevocably. God's salvation finds expression in the life of Jesus and reaches fulfillment in the free acceptance of death which recapitulates this life. That Jesus truly is the absolute bringer of salvation is established by God's vindication of Jesus in the resurrection. We are saved because in one of us God's salvation has been made present historically, explicitly and irrevocably.

In Jesus, his life, death and resurrection, we have an unambiguous sign of the positive outcome of history. In this case the death and resurrection are the sacramental cause of the salvation offered to all men and women. This sacramental sign is brought about by the saving will of God. The death and resurrection are the definitive historical expression of this will to save. What is signified, God's salvation, comes to be in and through the sign. In this sense the cross of Jesus is truly the cause of our salvation.

The Second Vatican Council can speak of the Church as the sacrament of the world's salvation. Rahner goes a step further and claims that Jesus Christ is the primary sacrament of salvation.[18] Through this approach of sacramental causality Karl Rahner manages to show how a single event in history may be seen to possess universal meaning, and be said to be the cause of the salvation that is offered to all men and women.

A Searching Christology

Rahner's line of thought seems to establish that men and women of all times, including non-believers, may be saved through God's free self-communication in Jesus Christ. But what about the human response? If non-believers may be saved by an implicit faith, does this implicit faith have any real connection to Jesus Christ? From God's side we can see that salvation is always given in and through Jesus Christ, even to those who have never heard of him. But from the human side we must ask whether the response to God on the part of those who have no explicit faith in Jesus nevertheless has a real relationship to the life, death and resurrection of Jesus of Nazareth.

Rahner believes that salvation is centered on Jesus Christ not only from the point of view of God's self-communication, but also from the point of view of the human faith response. He holds this to be true both when a person has explicit faith in Christian revelation and also when a person has no access to the Christian Gospel and has only an implicit faith. In this second case Rahner would argue that those who have never heard of Jesus Christ are, in fact, engaged in a "Christology of quest."

A person who has never heard the Gospel and who is responding to God's self-communication by obedience to conscience is already saved by God and responding by grace to God with supernatural (implicit) faith. This free assent of faith implies a willingness to accept the fullness of God's self-revelation. A person in this situation is engaged in a quest for Jesus Christ in the sense that his or her existence is grace-filled, and this grace finds its historical and tangible expression only in Jesus Christ. The person whose life is centered on grace is prepared to accept the goal of this grace, and the goal of this grace is Jesus Christ. All human beings under grace are in a pilgrim state, searching for the meaning of what has been given in grace.

According to Rahner "a person who is searching for something which is specific and yet unknown has a genuine existential connection, as one alert and on the watch, with whatever he is seeking, even if he has not yet found it, and so cannot develop the relation to the object of his quest to its full extent."[19] Such a connection is sufficient for us to say that a person who does not have explicit faith in Jesus Christ may yet have a real connection with him. The connection exists in that Jesus is the goal of the quest which is at the heart of the person's life. Because of God's self-communication, mysteriously encountered and accepted, the person is necessarily engaged upon such a quest. Unlike the Christian who believes in the Gospel such a person does not know that what he or she seeks is to be found in Jesus of Nazareth.

Rahner believes, then, that "if a person accepts his existence resolutely, he is already living out in his existence something like a 'searching Christology.' "[20] He finds that illustrated in three aspects of human existence: the appeal to an absolute love of neighbor, the appeal to readiness for death, and the appeal to hope in the future.

In our human experience of love for another person we can find something absolute and unconditional. Our love has a radical character that drives it beyond what is safe. In spite of the unreliability and finite character of the human person our human love risks itself absolutely for another. Rahner argues that this love which gives itself unconditionally to another "affirms Christ implicitly in faith and love."[21] Such a love is searching for the infinite God, but it is also searching for one who may be loved as a concrete human person. It is love searching for Jesus Christ. All human persons are inter-related and our love tends to reach out and embrace all others. Rahner argues on the one hand that our love for another opens up in searching toward the love of Jesus

Christ. On the other hand the existence of one who is "God-man" within the single human race makes possible the absolute love of another human person.

A second area of human existence in which we can find a "searching Christology" is the facing of death. When a free person willingly accepts the powerlessness of death, and this is not simply the acceptance of the absurd, then such a person faces death with some element of expectant hope. There is hope, writes Rahner, that death is of such a nature "that it reconciles the permanent dialectic in us between doing and enduring in powerlessness."[22] A person who surrenders to death in this way is already "searching" for that which can bring meaning to the experience of death, and this reality is the death and resurrection of Jesus.

In a similar way our experience of hope in the future opens us up toward a "searching" Christology. We hope to overcome the alienation we experience, and to lessen the gap between what we are and what we would like to be. If we dare hope for an absolute reconciliation, and if we dare hope that this belongs to human history and history is moving toward this goal, then hope is directed toward Jesus Christ, understood as the absolute future of human history.

Rahner would say, then, that a person who radically loves another, willingly accepts death, or hopes in the future is searching for the absolute Savior.[23] This is true whether a person is explicitly aware of this search or not. This search is part of life because human existence is transformed by grace.

3
Gustavo Gutierrez

Gustavo Gutierrez does his theology from the perspective of the oppressed peoples of Latin America. Like other theologians engaged in constructing "liberation theology" he attempts to reflect theologically in solidarity with the poor. Gutierrez is important for this book not only because of his significance in the development of Latin American theology, but because he has treated systematically the theme of the inner relationship between human liberation and salvation in Jesus Christ. He has constructed a contemporary theology of salvation. This theology is developed from the point of view of marginalized peoples in Latin America, but it has significance for the whole Church. I will outline Gutierrez's position by discussing first his theological method, then his view of liberation and salvation, and finally some aspects of his thought on spirituality.

Theology from the Underside of History

Because Gutierrez is critically aware of the social function of religion and theology, he is necessarily concerned about method in theology.[1] Two insights characterize his theological method: (1) theology is a "second step," and (2) theology must be done from the perspective of the poor. Without excluding other approaches to theology, Gutierrez consistently sees his own theology as a "second step" or a "second act."[2] The first step is ecclesial pastoral action, or engagement in the struggle for human liberation. Theology follows action. Theology, for Gutierrez, is critical reflection on praxis in the light of the word of God.[3] Theology then has a critical and prophetic function. It offers a basis for criticism of both social order and Church life. It interprets historical events seeking to make manifest their most profound meaning. Theology is critical thinking from within a situation of engagement. It is the second step: "What Hegel used to say about philosophy can likewise be applied to theology: it rises only at sundown."[4]

According to Gutierrez (and, of course, many other contemporary thinkers) theology is always tied to social processes. A theology arises as part of an historical context and mind-set, and it cannot be understood if it is divorced from them.[5] No theology is politically neutral. Like all systems of thought, theology is socially conditioned, and performs a social function. A theology becomes critically effective only when this is taken into account. A critically aware theology has the capacity to challenge the social and political order.

Gutierrez situates European theologies, including progressive political theologies like that of J.B. Metz, against the background of the Enlightenment. The Industrial Revolution, the intellectual Enlightenment, the French Revolution, the quest for individual freedom and the rise of scientific thinking shape the context for European theology. These historical circumstances have given rise to the modern bourgeois spirit which challenges Christianity with rationalism and a skeptical approach to religion. Christian theology has had to cope with agnosticism and unbelief. At the same time Christianity has been increasingly relegated to the private sphere and ceased having much impact in the public life of politics and economics. Gutierrez shows how this context shapes the best of twentieth century theology in Europe and North

America, as theologians grapple with non-belief on the one hand and with the need to develop a critical political theology on the other.[6]

Liberation theology is consciously articulated from a radically different context. Its context is the misery of millions of exploited men and women, and the fact that these people are increasingly becoming aware of their own situation, and becoming part of an historical movement of social change. The rise of the middle class in some parts of the world is linked with the exploitation of the poorest in other parts of the world. As the domination and degradation of the American Indian once enriched Europeans, so today the poverty and hunger of millions in Latin America is linked to those who profit from the wealth of huge multi-national companies. It is the exploited groups, the silent ones whose history is repressed, who make up the "underside" of history.[7] It is from this underside of history that Gutierrez seeks to do his theological reflection.

Although there is creative dialogue between Latin American liberation theology and progressive European theology, there is also a real difference between them. The difference emerges when the question is asked: With whom are the two theologies in dialogue? Progressive European theology is in dialogue with the modern spirit, with the middle class non-believer. Liberation theology, by contrast, is in dialogue with the "non-person," the "non-human."[8] A theology engaged with the "non-person" is necessarily different from a theology engaged with the "non-believer." The questions addressed to theology from the excluded and the poor have to do with economics and politics. These are not immediately religious issues, but that does not mean that they are not significant for Christian faith or Christian theology. On the contrary the judgment scene of Matthew 25 shows that they are of final significance. Gutierrez quotes Berdyaev on this issue: "If I am hungry, that is a material problem; if someone else is hungry, that is a spiritual problem."[9]

Gutierrez attempts to do theology from the perspective of those who have been made non-persons. He does not mean to suggest that he is unique in his attempt to do theology from the underside. Rather he argues that the perspective of the poor has often broken in upon Church life and Christian theology. Like subterranean streams that gush up here and there, the faith experience of the poor has emerged in history. Contemporary theology has to study these moments. It needs to reread history from the side of the poor, and to construct a theology for today that is in continuity with the memory of the poor of history.

Several times Gutierrez refers to a text from Bonhoeffer:

> It is an experience of incomparable value to have learned to see the great events of the history of the world from beneath: from the viewpoint of the useless, the suspect, the abused, the powerless, the oppressed, the despised—in a word, from the viewpoint of those who suffer.[10]

A theology which takes this stance can be seen as "an expression of the right to think of the wretched of the earth."[11] If this is to be so the theologian cannot simply reflect in an ivory tower. The theologian needs to be involved not only in the "second act" but also in the "first act," the praxis of liberation and the celebration of the word in relationship to that praxis. Then it may be said that the theologian is a "thinker with organic links to the popular liberation undertaking, and with the Christian communities that live their faith by taking this historical task upon themselves as their own."[12]

Doing theology from the underside means taking sides in a conflict-ridden situation. Repeatedly Gutierrez insists that we are not faithful to the Gospels when we pretend that conflict does not exist, or when we choose to attempt to be neutral when one group is crushing another. Such "neutrality" in fact supports the oppression. There is no contradiction between an option for the oppressed classes and the Gospel call to universal love. Gutierrez argues that a Christian must love those who belong to oppressive and exploiting groups. This love is shown, he argues, by struggling with the poor against them. Love for those who exploit is shown in opposing their actions and policies. Solidarity with the poor is the only way to practice universal love in a conflict-ridden situation.

Gutierrez attempts to develop a theology which faithfully announces the Gospel, which is a reflection on practice, and which is done in solidarity with the poor. This approach characterizes all his work.[13] Already it says much about Gutierrez's approach to the question of salvation. In his foundation work, *A Theology of Liberation,* we find this theme of salvation explored explicitly.

Liberation and Salvation

The most fundamental question addressed by Gutierrez in his *A Theology of Liberation* is: What relationship is there between salvation in Jesus Christ and the historical process of the liberation of women and men? This is related to the question about the connection between faith and existence in the world, a question which appears today when our contempories ask about the connection between the kingdom of God and our own efforts in building up the world. More particularly, for Gutierrez, it is the question about the relationship between faith and political action. In our history we see the emergence of a human person who is conscious of being an active agent in history. Effective political action is not an optional extra for such a person; rather the construction of a society in which people can live in solidarity and freedom is seen as central to human existence in the world. This kind of social and political action involves a person in a public arena which is necessarily conflictual. From this perspective Gutierrez asks about the meaning of salvation in Jesus Christ.

Gutierrez considers three ways in which Christians have han-

dled the connection between faith and politics.[14] The first of these
is the "Christendom" approach in which the Church experienced
itself as a powerful force in relationship to the world. In this view
the Church was the only arena of salvation, and the Church
seemed almost co-extensive with the known world. In the long
history of Christendom, "temporal realities" lacked any real autonomy; society and politics were thought of as being at the service of the Church and the Church's mission. Christians who
worked in government and other temporal tasks were expected to
work for the benefit of the Church. In the Christendom mentality
faith and society were bound together in an intimate union.

In this century we have had to come to terms with the fact
that the intimate union between Church and politics has come to
an end. Jacques Maritain attempted a new approach to the relationship between Church life and the "temporal sphere." In his
view (called "New Christendom") the autonomy of the secular
sphere is asserted. The hierarchy have no right to interfere beyond
their competence. The layperson takes on the function of acting
in the world according to Christian principles, attempting to build
a "New Christendom" inspired by these principles.

A third approach, called by Gutierrez the "Distinction of
Planes," was soon to follow. Now the secular world was seen as
even more autonomous. Church life was seen as revolving around
two missions, evangelization and the inspiration of the temporal
sphere. Inspired by Congar's earlier writings a clear distinction
was made between the mission to evangelize and build up the
Church on the one hand, and the mission to inspire the temporal
order on the other. The mission of the ordained minister was ecclesial; the minister was to evangelize and to inspire the temporal
order, but not become actively involved in it. The layperson, on
the other hand, had the responsibility to work for a more just and
more human society in the world. The approach is behind much
of the fruitful work of those lay apostolate groups which took on
the "Review of Life" method. It is also found in many of the texts

of Vatican II, although *Gaudium et Spes* goes beyond the rigid distinction of the two planes. What unites the two planes is a theology that God's kingdom involves both the Church and the building of a more just and more human society.

For various reasons this sharp distinction between Church and world, and between ordained and lay Christians, has been called into question. Lay apostolate groups which have tried to operate in this way have found that when they take a stand on an issue it tends to involve Church leaders. As some of these groups have become more political their positions have put them at odds with the hierarchy. In the difficulties and frustrations that have followed many of these groups have ceased to function. On the other hand a growing understanding of the misery of the poor has led many ordained ministers to abandon a policy of non-intervention, and they have taken a strongly committed position. These pastoral realities call for a new theological reflection. As Gutierrez sees it, the kind of position taken by the Latin American bishops at Medellín requires a new theological foundation.

The pastoral need for a new theology of salvation emerges even more clearly from Gutierrez's description of the historical process of liberation that is taking place in Latin America, and from his outline of the Church's experience of itself in the process of liberation.[15] This unique faith experience demands a new attempt at understanding the theology of salvation. Added to this pastoral requirement there is a new theological context. The old, clear distinction between nature and grace has largely disappeared, and we are conscious today that all men and women live in a world of grace and are invited into communion with the Lord. There is a divine vocation offered to all. We are all invited to receive the gift of salvation. In this new theological context the dividing lines between faith and temporal works are no longer so clear. This approach suggests that we might see our action in history as the place where God's salvation occurs. Salvation, which Gutierrez sees as communion with God and communion amongst ourselves, can now be seen as an event which transforms and guides our history to its fulfillment. There is but one human history, and "the history of salvation is the very heart of human history."[16] Our one human history has been irreversibly assumed by Christ.

Gutierrez moves toward a more profound understanding of salvation through a reflection on the close link in the Scriptures between God's creation and the experience of God's salvation in the exodus event.[17] In the Bible, creation is seen as the first salvific act, as part of God's salvation. The same God is Creator and Redeemer. The Creator of the world is Israel's Liberator. The liberation of the people can also be seen as a new creation in which God frees this people in order to take them into covenant love. Creation is seen as the first saving action, and salvation is seen as a new creation. In Christ this movement comes to fulfillment. The work of Jesus is seen in terms of a new creation. It is also seen in terms of liberation from sin and all its consequences. All things have been created in Jesus Christ and in him all are saved.

If we are to understand salvation in these terms, then it is highly significant that in the account of creation the human person is called to continue the work of creation through labor, and that in God's liberation of the chosen people in the exodus it is through human political action that God's salvation is accomplished. The mediating factor which enables us to grasp the profound relationship between God's creation and salvation is the "self-creation" of the human person. Through labor, through building up community, through struggling against misery and exploitation, through working for a just society, we create ourselves. Yet this self-creation is also the gift of a free God who creates and saves us. The biblical view of creation and salvation insists that our human efforts are a continuation of the work of creation, and that God's salvation, which is always a free gift, is the "inner force" and the "fullness" of our own action to transform our world.[18]

Gutierrez's thinking about salvation is further developed as he reflects about the biblical theme of the eschatological promises. What we find throughout the Scriptures is a tension between the implementation of promises in the present and the direction toward a fuller implementation in the future. Moreover the driving force toward the future arises in and through the partial fulfillment of the present. This means that what we have are "partial fulfillments through liberating historical events which are in turn new promises marking the road toward total fulfillment."[19] This line of thought provides the possibility of showing how liberating action might be a partial realization of salvation from God, without being identified with salvation from God. The promises of God are being fulfilled through our history, but they cannot be identified with this or that event. They always open up beyond the present to new and unforeseen possibilities.

From his study of these two biblical themes Gutierrez emerges with two key ideas for his theology of liberation. On the one hand from his study of the theme of creation and salvation he shows that God's free gift of salvation is given in and through human action, as its inner force and final goal. On the other hand from his study of the theme of the eschatological promises he shows how our human activity may be a partial realization of God's salvation, but it can never be identified with it.

For Gutierrez the theology of salvation has to be such that it makes sense to third world peoples who find themselves in an "oppression-liberation axis."[20] The context which concerns him is the exploitation of huge masses of people, the conflict between social classes, and the movement toward political liberation. This approach opens up new ways of understanding sin. The Medellín Conference had described the state of affairs in Latin America as a "sinful situation." Gutierrez regards sin as a social, historical fact, the absence of community and love in relationships, and a breach of friendship with God and between persons. Because of this it is also an interior personal fracture.[21] Sin is painfully evident in social and political structures: in oppressive economic structures, in domination and slavery of classes or races, in all kinds of exploitation. Sin, then, is at the root of injustice. This means that an unjust situation demands the redemption from sin that we are offered in Christ, and this redemption implies also the necessity of real political liberation. Sinful social and political situations call for the liberation which comes only in the forgiving grace of God, and this implies action to change the unjust situation.

In fact, Gutierrez distinguishes three levels of meaning of the single complex process of liberation.[22] All three levels are interdependent and interrelated. First there is political liberation. At this level liberation expresses the hopes of oppressed peoples and oppressed classes who are trapped in a conflictual situation of exploitation. Second there is the liberation of humanity throughout history. Here liberation points to the unfolding of all the dimensions of human life, providing a vision of a new person and a new social order. Third, at the deepest level liberation means freedom from sin and admission to communion with God. These three levels are all part of a single salvific process. They are mutually interconnected, so that one is not present without the others. However, they are distinct and must not be confused.

If sin is the root of injustice then the reign of God is the precondition for a just society. However, the reign of God cannot be reduced to human progress. God's salvation cannot be identified with this or that project. When we act for justice, attempting to overcome our selfishness in an effort to live in love, we can say that such participation in the struggle for human liberation "is a salvific work, although it is not all of salvation."[23]

God's liberation is necessary if we are truly to overcome sinful structures. However God's liberation occurs historically in and through our own efforts at human liberation. But God's liberation always transcends our human projects: "While liberation is implemented in liberating historical events, it also denounces their limitations and ambiguities, proclaims their fulfillment, and impels them effectively toward total communion.''[24] The historical liberating event, then, ''*is* the growth of the Kingdom and *is* a salvific event; however, it is not *the* coming of the Kingdom, nor all of salvation.''[25] It is an historical realization of the kingdom which points beyond itself and proclaims the fullness of the kingdom.

For Gutierrez, then, Jesus Christ is the Liberator whose saving action embraces all levels of human existence. His liberating activity cannot be reduced only to a religious dimension of life. It touches the basic structure of personal and political life. Salvation in Christ is a radical liberation from all misery and all oppression. It encompasses all three levels of liberation. Through Jesus Christ salvation is present at the heart of human history.

Spirituality and Human Liberation

In his recent book, *We Drink from Our Own Wells,* Gutierrez tentatively describes what he sees as characteristic features of the spirituality that is emerging among those who are engaged in the struggle for liberation in Latin America. While keeping in mind the circular relationship between experience and the Gospel message, he seeks to express what is distinctive in the experience of these Christians. He links characteristics of this emerging spirituality in five couples, arguing that the interconnections help us to understand the experience more precisely: (1) conversion as a requirement for solidarity; (2) gratuitousness as the atmosphere for efficacy; (3) joy as victory over suffering; (4) spiritual childhood as a requirement for commitment to the poor; (5) community out of solitude.

This outline of a spirituality of liberation is a significant complement to the theology of liberation already discussed. In terms of a theology of salvation it is obviously important to consider how salvation is actually experienced. In his articulation of these five themes Gutierrez is describing the way God's salvation is in fact being experienced by Christians engaged in the process of liberation.

The first theme that Gutierrez discusses is that of conversion. Those who seek to be in solidarity with the poor find themselves constantly called to conversion. This ongoing conversion calls for a break from sin, and this sin has both personal and social dimensions: "The encounter with the Lord in the inmost recesses of the individual does not exclude but rather calls for a similar encounter in the depths of the wretchedness in which the poor of our countries live."[26] The invitation to conversion comes from the suffering features of Christ that can be recognized in the poor. The conversion required means a recognition of our participation in injustice, and it calls for a break with the social milieu to which we belong. It is a call to a new world, the world of the poor. The experience of solidarity with the poor is at the same time a call to profound conversion to Jesus Christ. It is not an option that a Christian takes alone, but rather something that a person seeks to do in solidarity with the whole Church. As the bishops at Puebla affirmed, there is a need for conversion of the whole Church to a preferential option for the poor. A real solidarity with the poor calls for real love and affection, for real tenderness directed toward human beings of flesh and blood. It also calls for a fidelity and a constancy, which Gutierrez calls "stubbornness," and this stubbornness is grounded in trust in the Lord.

A second element in this spirituality is the experience of gratuity at the heart of the process of liberation. Authentic Christian love must seek to transform unjust situations by effective action. However, it is a mistake to suppose that the search for effective action and the experience that "everything is grace" are opposites. Neither can they be simply made into a synthesis. Rather, Gutierrez suggests, gratuity is the atmosphere in which the quest for effectiveness is bathed. It is in the attempt at effective action that many Latin Americans experience that all of life is a gift. Effective action must be seen to take place in a fully human context, and "that context is the space of freely bestowed encounter with the Lord." The experience of gratuity opens up the possibility of the contemplative dimension in life. It finds expression in the silence of prayer. Gutierrez comments: "It is surprising to see a people becoming increasingly better organized and more effective in the struggle to assert its rights to life and justice and at the same time giving evidence of a profound sense of prayer and of a conviction that in the final analysis love and peace are an unmerited gift from God."[27] Gutierrez insists, with Matthew 25:31–46, that we truly encounter Christ in the earthiness of our encounter with the poor. However, he suggests that a true and full encounter with the neighbor requires that we first experience the gratuity of God's love. Once this love is experienced as a gift, then "our approach to others is purified of any tendency to impose an alien will on them; it is disinterested and respectful of their personalities, their needs and aspirations."[28]

Joy in spite of suffering is a third element in this emerging spirituality. This is not a superficial rejoicing that comes from resignation to evil, but the paschal joy of those committed to overcoming injustice. Such joy is not a refusal to face the misery and degradation of so many. It is the paradoxical experience of life and hope that is shared by those who face the horror of poverty and its causes and together search for effective action. There is failure and pain in all of this and there is the growing list of martyrs who have given their lives in love for God and for the poor. Gutierrez points out that this experience of martyrdom is something "that happens but is not sought."[29] It happens only in the cause of the affirmation of life. The experience of hope amidst the suffering of the poor and the martyrdom of so many brings a new meaning to the Easter message. Gutierrez cites what a Christian activist wrote from prison: "Everytime I am threatened by bitterness or anguish, I feel the presence of God and all of you supporting me, and then I want only to rejoice."[30] Struggle against misery costs much, but those who engage in the struggle find their lives touched by a paschal joy, which comes as a gift given at the heart of the struggle.

The fourth theme is the necessity of "spiritual childhood" for those who would enter into solidarity with the poor. Gutierrez insists that the Christian response to the fact of poverty is solidarity with the poor and opposition to the poverty that afflicts them. Poverty must not be spiritualized. On the contrary it must be rejected as evil. Voluntary poverty, detachment from material goods, has meaning only within the perspective of real commitment to the poor. This means a real entering the world of the poor: "It means being one of its inhabitants, looking upon it as a place of residence and not simply of work." Gutierrez reflects on the experience of those who have attempted this kind of solidarity. There is the experience that the poor are flesh and blood, subject to grace but also to sin and selfishness. There is the experience that one can only approach the world of the poor, without ever reaching the point of real identification with them. There is also the danger of a kind of triumphalism and new self-righteousness on the part of those who would enter the world of the poor. All of this means that spiritual childhood is required of those who would be in solidarity with marginalized people. An early insight for liberation theology had been that poverty of spirit, in the sense of detachment from riches, can have meaning only in the context of solidarity with the poor. Now Gutierrez argues that poverty of spirit, in the sense of spiritual childhood, is an indispensable condition for authentic commitment to the poor. This is not a theoretical truth but something that emerges from the experience of many. This spiritual childhood finds its permanent model in Mary and in her Magnificat. Latin American Christians find a combination of a "trusting self-surrender to God with a will to commitment and close association with God's favorites: the lowly, the hungry."[31]

Finally, there is the experience of solitude and of community in the struggle for liberation. There is a real suffering and loneliness which emerges amongst those who identify with the poor. There is a "dark night" that can occur amidst the struggle against hopelessness and overwhelming odds. There is also the discovery of real solitude, of a real taste of God in the depths of the "dark night of injustice." This solitude has nothing to do with individualism. On the contrary it opens up a hunger for communion, and it is a condition for real community: "There is an aloneness with oneself and with God that, however hard it may be to endure at certain times, is a requirement for authentic community."[32] Solitude and community are not to be seen as successive stages of life, but they are both related at a more profound and mysterious level. It is within community that we experience solitude and it is community life that sustains us for solitude. The Eucharist holds central place in such a community life, celebrating a hope for the future which motivates present commitments. Gutierrez can affirm that an "ecclesial outlook is one of the dominant notes of the spirituality now coming to birth in Latin America."[33]

4
Sebastian Moore

While other theologians move from one aspect of theology to another Sebastian Moore has been working consistently at understanding the experience of salvation in Jesus Christ. His theology is very much "work in progress" and I shall attempt to follow the development of his thought through three of his recent books.[1]

The Crucified Is No Stranger

In *The Crucified Is No Stranger* Sebastian Moore is concerned with articulating what happens when a contemporary believer is confronted with the cross of Jesus. The book is written in dialogue with the understanding of the human person that comes from depth psychology. Above all Moore is attempting a theological response to Ernest Becker's book *The Denial of Death*.[2] Becker's work is a brilliant attempt at a contemporary anthropology, written in full consciousness of existential philosophy and depth psychology, particularly that of Otto Rank.

Becker sees the human person as always having a need to stand out as central and significant from other reality. There is a universal need to be "heroic," to find a cosmic significance for the self. The other side of this need for significance is the terror

46

of death. Against the fear of non-existence the human person has to establish the self as meaningful. According to Becker the terror of death is so powerful that if we allowed ourselves to experience it consciously we would be unable to function normally. We have to repress the fear of death in order to live in the everyday world. Human character, then, is a "vital lie."[3] We need to repress what we are unable to handle in order to live successfully. Becker notes that a boy growing up learns "how life is really too much for him, how he has to avoid too much thought, too much perception, too much *life*," and "how he has to avoid the death that rumbles behind and underneath every carefree activity, that looks over his shoulder as he plays."[4] In order to live life comfortably we have to guard ourselves from too much life as well as from death. We do this by cutting life down to size and admitting to consciousness only what we can handle.

Because of our desire to assert ourselves in relationship to the world and because of our fear of too much life and death, we have a need to unburden ourselves by finding a meaning outside ourselves. We seek meaning and wholeness in something or someone. We transfer onto this other reality the qualities we do not realize in ourselves. Relationship with this object then gives a sense of security and well-being. According to Becker this process of projection is not an aberration but a necessity for human life. It is the human attempt at wholeness, at finding a source of healing. It is obvious enough that all kinds of unworthy realities can become that which gives meaning to human existence. The real question then becomes: What is creative projection?

At the heart of all of this is the unwillingness to accept creaturehood and vulnerability. Because of the need to establish one's self and the need to prove that "I am somebody" over against the chaos of death and non-existence, a human person can end up destroying others. If another person undermines whatever makes us feel significant, and beyond death, then we are liable to hit back violently. We deny our finitude and vulnerability, and then we

desperately defend the structures of denial. Sebastian Moore
brings this understanding of human reality into a theological confrontation with the cross of Jesus. Moore sees this whole denial
of self and of the self's potential as being part of the sinful condition of human existence. We find ourselves caught in a great,
unconscious refusal. What are we refusing? According to Moore
we are refusing the fullness of life, the call to become fully ourselves. Behind this refusal is the all-pervasive fear that is connected to the mystery of evil in human existence. In a later book
Sebastian Moore will "retract" the view that sin can be identified
with this deeply rooted fear. However, there is no denying that
fear and refusal of life do have a relationship with sin and evil even
though they do not explain all of what sin is. The refusal of life
shows itself in the resentment that is felt in the presence of an ex-
ceptional and good person, and in the desire to get rid of such a
challenge to mediocrity. Fear of life and fear of our creaturehood
means that we tend to obliterate whatever reminds us of either of
those realities.

In *The Crucified Is No Stranger* Sebastian Moore's concern
is not so much with the historical event of the life and death of
Jesus as with the experience of the believer today confronted by
the cross of Jesus. His question, then, is: What happens when a
Christian is confronted in meditation, in liturgy, and in the daily
living of discipleship with Jesus crucified?

The answer to this question brings us to the heart of Moore's
argument. The diffuse evil which is part of everybody's life, although repressed from conscious awareness, is made conscious
and explicit before the cross. As we confront the victim on the
cross, we become aware that we are willful destroyers and cru-
cifiers. We are destroyers of our true selves. We crucify the vulnerable sinless one before us because we fear the vulnerability in
ourselves.

Evil then becomes recognized, and known as sin. This step
of recognition of the fact that I am a sinful crucifier is absolutely

vital in Sebastian Moore's argument. However, of itself it would lead only to despair. When it occurs in the context of God's overwhelming mercy and love, then there is the experience of redemption. Before the cross of Jesus "evil becomes sin and sin becomes forgiveness."[5] Before the crucified we experience ourselves unmasked, and our unmasked selves as accepted and loved. The attempt at self-sufficiency gives way to sorrow and the experience of conversion. We know ourselves at our worst, and yet that worst is forgiven and healed.

Sebastian Moore argues that today we have a new title for Jesus. He is "the self."[6] Through the action of the Holy Spirit we become conscious of the inner core of our humanity and are able to identify this self with Jesus. This self transcends the part of our beings that we are conscious of, and can be seen as the place where Jesus calls each person to personhood and freedom. Jesus on the cross represents an identity which we crucify rather than enter. However, the very act of destruction brings my true self out into the open: "Forced to hear myself saying 'I hate that which makes for life, I expose myself to sorrow, and sorrow, if I give it free reign, bears me in to the heart of the crucified where I discover myself.' "[7] In this conversion the believer passes over from being a crucifier to being identified with Christ crucified. Conversion, through sorrow, "consists in shifting my position from the crucifying ego to the crucified self."[8]

Human beings turn evil against themselves. They fear themselves. They crucify themselves. All this becomes explicit in confrontation with the sinless one upon the cross. This truth becomes bearable only through the power of the love expressed in the cross. My self-hatred reaches its climax and its resolution when faced with the love of God revealed in the death of Jesus.

In this experience of the crucified not only are we forgiven, but this forgiveness leads to a new view of death. Since we need no longer pretend that we are infinite and eternal we are freed from our old view of death. Death is transformed in Jesus' death and resurrection. It can now be seen for what it is—"return to the Father."[9] As we acknowledge ourselves as sinners "we find our identity in the man our sin has crucified, and in him, know death as the Father's embrace."[10] The concept of death is transformed in the experience of forgiveness. The source of so much of the fear that pervades our lives is transformed.

When the divine forgiveness breaks in upon life it begins to dissolve the system of self-awareness whereby we are either "euphoric" or "depressed." When someone offers us a challenge to our way of acting or thinking we tend either to reject it in our attempt to hold on to our inflated (and euphoric) view of ourselves, or to accept it in a depressed and self-pitying way. We demand worship from others, because we cannot face our mortality. When worship is refused we easily crash from euphoria to depression.

This awareness opens up what Moore calls an "ascetico-mystical" program. This means a constant contemplation of Jesus in life. When this is done we often find that what at first seemed "life's crucifixion of me" is in reality "my crucifixion of life." Sebastian Moore writes: "The question 'who is crucifying whom? what is crucifying what?', asked prayerfully and reflectively, is, I find, a talisman for liberating my friends from my tyranny and liberating myself from this tyranny."[11] The ego thinks it is badly done by, until I discover that it is the ego that is making demands and crucifying. Once this discovery is made, I can identify with the crucified self, with truth.

At the end of *The Crucified Is No Stranger* Sebastian Moore tells a story. I cite the story in full since it is an effective summary of much of the book and because it is a story to which many people can relate.

> I was giving a course of lectures which, so far as I could judge, were going very well. One day a close friend asked me 'how was this morning's class?' 'Good', I replied, 'they're

really the best lot I've had'. He replied that he had overheard
a few members of the class saying they hadn't a clue where
I was going and were very frustrated. I went to my room, and
sat like a stone. Although I had a talk to give in an hour, I
could not turn my mind to it. I was dead, destroyed, and angry.

After about half an hour I thought vaguely of the cross and
the new thoughts I was beginning to have about it. In connection with the painful experience I had just had, I began to
ask 'what's going on here?' Somehow the suggestion then
formed itself (and not in answer to the question 'who's crucifying whom?', because that question only came into my
system as a result of this experience) that, contrary to my feeling of being crucified by my friend's information, it was my
ego, with its inveterate euphoria, that was the crucifier, the
class—or rather the true situation between the class and myself—the crucified. Euphoria is a great destroyer of life with
its vast variety of tones and shades. It will have everything to
be going splendidly—or else it will resign. Meanwhile life is
trying to breathe. This student has understood. That one has
not. That other one thinks he has, and has understood something else. And so on. But the ego will have none of this. And
its first target—though not easily spotted—is my self, my
body, the actual communications that are going out to those
men and women.

With this thought I began to revive, with a new feeling for
my class, for myself, and for life. In an hour I knew that I
had made for me a very important discovery.[12]

The Fire and the Rose Are One

If the central focus of *The Crucified Is No Stranger* is the
experience of the contemporary believer confronted by the cross

of Jesus, in *The Fire and the Rose Are One* Sebastian Moore shifts his attention to the historical event of the death of Jesus, and to his victory over death, as these were experienced by the disciples of Jesus. He now finds that it is through a study of the experience of the disciples that we are led to a deeper grasp of the mystery of salvation.

The first two sections of the book are a reworking of Moore's anthropology, as he answers the question: What do we look for in ourselves by which to recognize Jesus?[13] In this new book the human person is understood not simply as someone directed toward freedom from guilt and fear, but as someone who is radically oriented toward God.

Moore builds his picture of the human person from what he takes to be the most fundamental and universal need, the need to feel significant. This need for significance reaches new intensity when I find myself attracted to another, and experience the desire that this other be attracted toward me. The need for significance finds its full meaning in the love for another, a love which creates happiness in the other. Moore suggests that a definition of the universal human need is "the need to be myself for another." In this definition the word "for" refers to both my attraction to the other, and the other's attraction to me. Other ways of expressing this basic proposition are "everyone wants to be attractive to someone whom he or she finds attractive," and "we all desire to be desired by one we desire."[14]

However the need for significance has its roots in the uncertainty that characterizes human existence. We do not know where we are going and we cannot account for our origin. As Becker has pointed out we are always attempting to deal with the fact that we need not exist by pretending we are immortal and that we create ourselves. Sebastian Moore's suggestion is that our need for significance is ultimately a need to know that we are significant to our origin. Furthermore, he suggests, this anxiety can be compared to what one feels when wondering what the beloved feels about oneself. A human person is one who is always asking "Am I significant in God's eyes?" even though the question may not be consciously expressed. This question has an urgency that is best understood in terms of our need to be loved.

Sebastian Moore is bringing together the basic experience that we are not self-sufficient with the experience of our hunger for meaning. Our mind tells us that we are contingent, that we need not exist. Our hearts long to hear a word which says we are loved. God is sought not only with the mind, but with the heart; in fact the mind and heart are one. There is a "pre-religious emotional involvement with God" at the heart of human existence.[15] Religious conversion, then, may be seen as the experience and the conviction that God does love us, that we are of significance to our origin.

Moore suggests that, even though the question we ask of a human person seems much more real than the question we ask of God, the question to God is the most basic characteristic of human existence. The need to know whether I have meaning for the mystery responsible for my existence is the driving force for everything else. The basic human need is a passionate hunger to hear the yes of that mysterious Beloved who is the source of existence.

The other side of our human existence is characterized by guilt and sin. Guilt is the sense of failing another. We recoil from another, withdraw into ourselves, and often experience the other person as ugly and unattractive. Moore suggests that this dislike masks the real feeling which is guilt. In relationship with God, guilt is a result of the sin of withdrawing from the source of all meaning into isolated self-awareness. Original sin consists in treating as non-existent our dependence on ultimate mystery; it has a social and cultural dimension since this "conspiratorial silence" becomes expressed in human institutions.[16]

Sin is the attempt to disengage oneself, to close off from the Other, to be "absolutely myself-for-myself-alone."[17] Guilt is the symptom of sin, a sense of failing God and others. At its core it

is a self-denial, a self-hatred. It is a refusal to come out of isolation. The forgiveness of sins is what enables us to come out of our
chosen isolation into the freedom of love.

With this anthropology in mind Sebastian Moore turns to the
Gospel story of Jesus. It is of central importance that we are told
that Jesus was without sin. If Jesus was the sinless one then he
was free of the negation that infects human life. He was incom-
parably free to be open to intimacy with God, startlingly free in
his relationships with women and men, and free to see that the
reign of God was breaking in upon the world in his own life and
ministry.

What effect would this kind of person have upon his followers? One who was sinless and free would have exercised a most
extraordinary attraction. The God whom the disciples came to
know through Jesus would have been so real and so vivid as to
make old religious convictions seem pale and empty by compar-
ison. It is true that the God of Jesus was the God of ancient Israel,
but it was this God mediated through one who was sinless. Jesus
enabled the disciples to experience the yes of God in an unparalleled way.

With the whole of their religious faith caught up in the ec-
static experience of following Jesus of Nazareth, the disciples
could experience his failure and tragic death only as the death of
God. The disciples, lifted so high by their life with Jesus, could
only be taken down to the depths of the Dark Night of the Soul in
the death of Jesus. If the closeness of God evoked by the company
of Jesus, the sinless one, is beyond our capacity to imagine, so,
too, is the sense of the death of God that occurred in Jesus' failure
and crucifixion.

Sebastian Moore argues that in this context the experience of
the risen Jesus involved a psychological "displacement" of divinity from the old God whom guilt had kept remote to the risen
Jesus. In Jesus they now experience what it is for God to be alive.
The risen Jesus is experienced as life, as outpouring of the Spirit,

as God's presence. This psychological displacement is the origin and foundation for the later formulations of the divinity of Jesus. In their resurrection experience the disciples encountered Jesus as doing what only God could do.

This awesome psychological experience of displacement was soon followed by a new, larger conceptual pattern whereby the old God became known as the Father who raises up the crucified, and "the prodigious divine vitality that cojoins the infinite mystery with a divine man is experienced, and named the Holy Spirit."[18] Thus Sebastian Moore holds that the Christological and Trinitarian statements of Nicaea and Chalcedon express something that is a matter of experience for the disciples. He holds that the way toward an appropriation of conciliar theology is through a discovery of the divinity of Jesus, which occurs as a disciple who has experienced the death of God meets the risen Lord. In the resurrection encounter "everything that will subsequently be doctrine is experience."[19]

There are three major developments between *The Crucified Is No Stranger* and *The Fire and the Rose Are One:* (1) the human person is seen as characterized by a pre-religious emotional relationship with God; (2) a more theological approach to sin and guilt replaces the psychological emphasis on fear; (3) the center of focus becomes the *disciples' experience* of the "Galilean Springtime," the death of Jesus and his resurrection.[20] These advances, however, do not invalidate the earlier work. While Moore may well be right in feeling that *The Crucified Is No Stranger* does not deal adequately with a profound view of sin, it does open up contemporary insights into what Paul meant by liberation from law. As well as teaching us about liberation from sin Paul argues in Galatians and Romans that the cross of Jesus liberates us from our need to establish ourselves as righteous. Depth psychology's discoveries are related to the Pauline doctrine that because of the death and resurrection of Jesus we are freed from the compulsion to prove ourselves right.

The Inner Loneliness

In the third book under consideration, *The Inner Loneliness,* Sebastian Moore continues to build his theology around the experience of the disciples of Jesus. However, he shifts the focus of his anthropology and comes to see the human person as characterized by a "cosmic loneliness."[21] This inner loneliness manifests itself above all in three areas of life: sexuality, earth-dependence and mortality. What the disciples of Jesus experienced, and what they communicated to the Church in the power of the Holy Spirit, is that this inner loneliness is dispelled by God in the death and resurrection of Jesus.

The human person, argues Moore, is self-aware even before there is explicit reflection on this fact. My self-awareness, he argues, is not so much my way of looking at myself, but rather my way of being with myself. It is this self-awareness that I manifest to another in human communication. This way of being with myself is also a self-love. Self-love and self-gift are closely connected: I want the self that I am aware of and love to be important to another.

This desire to be for another is only partially satisfied in any human relationship. No one can truly know me as I am in my self-awareness. No one can meet the hunger within me fully. If this inner need were to be met it could be done only by the ultimate mystery that grounds all of existence, a being that knows me from within, yet is other than myself, a being that is without limits and so infinitely capable of receiving me. Out of the human need to share self-awareness, Moore comes to a definition of God: "God is the other within that ends an otherwise ineluctable inner loneliness."[22] We human beings desire Another whose very "to be" is "to be for me."[23] We desperately desire a companion who is other than ourselves yet infinitely involved with us.

If self-love flowers only in self-giving to another, then our greatest happiness and pleasure is found in other-enhancement.

Moore argues that in this we participate in the reality of God for whom "to be" is "to love." God is the happy, joyful source of happiness in us. Moore quotes Meister Eckhart: "God enjoys himself and wants us to join him."[24] We have the desire to be for another in an unlimited way, and this is also a desire for limitless happiness. This desire, according to Moore, is grounded in a God who is a "limitless act of enjoyment which by being happy creates and nurtures and fosters and promotes."[25]

Sebastian Moore connects his view of the God who answers our inner loneliness with the philosophical tradition which describes God as the origin and source of all that exists. God is the one who by nature accounts for all of reality. In Aquinas' phrase God is *ipsum esse subsistens*. Moore paraphrases this as *"the idea of being, as itself being."*[26] This description of God as the cause of all that exists is brought into dialogue with the inner loneliness. Then God is seen as the one who by nature is concerned with my existence. The lonely human person desires that there be one who by nature is person and friend in an unlimited way. My lonely self-awareness is grounded in one who is the idea of me and of all reality, existing.

If the human person is constituted so that self-love flowers in self-gift, then a person whose self-love is not repressed can go to others without fear and enter into relationships with security. Where self-love is repressed and unacknowledged it generates insecurity and a compulsive need to dominate others. Sebastian Moore writes that "everyone experiences two forms of the central desire: the desire to relate—stemming from unrepressed self-love—and the desire to control—stemming from repressed/unavowed self-love."[27] Moore attributes evil, and the sense of guilt, to this split between self-love and self-gift.

Self-love is meant to send us out into creative relationships, and it is meant, too, to lead us in the direction of the transcendent companion. When self-love is repressed, and when it loses its connection with love for others, it leads to evil. Sebastian Moore explores this further by a discussion of human sexuality. He sees our sexuality as conditioned by a split between desire and the need for control. While in a primitive culture desire and control are connected creatively through the incest taboo, in contemporary culture the difficulty is handled through sexual repression.

Moore sees history as characterized by three great periods.[28] First there was matriarchal society characterized by tribally taught sexuality and the incest taboo. Second there is the patriarchal age, characterized by the search for male identity and spirituality, and also by the repression of sexuality. We are currently at the dawn of a new age in which women will seek to find their own identity, and lead us beyond the old matriarchy and our experience of the patriarchal age toward new possibilities for human existence. Men in the patriarchal age have been driven to search for the meaning of their incompleteness. In the process they have dominated and abused women. At times they have found their male identity beyond women in God. The problem here is that men have tended to make God male and use God to endorse dominance over women. As women, in this new age, bring their search for sexual identity toward the center of the cultural stage, new possibilities appear for a more whole spirituality.

Moore argues that the sexuality that drives both men and women in search of identity is in reality a yearning for God. The inner loneliness, which our sexuality reminds us of constantly, is a craving for the absolute friend and lover. When our sexual loneliness is out of touch with God, then the immediate effect is awkwardness and disorder. The problem is not the loss of control of our desires but the loss of friendship with our desires: ''Sexuality is out of control *because* it is unbefriended, and this is the *meaning* of lust.''[29]

My sexuality, and my body, raise a question about who I am. The question is urgent, but there is no answer. The opposite sex does not provide the final answer. I am forced to face the question of meaning alone. Not only sexuality, but dependence on earth for survival, and the fact of mortality, force us to face the issue of our loneliness, what Moore calls cosmic loneliness. He argues that, "unrelieved," this loneliness is the root of all human evil. When it is relieved in the love of God it is the source of all good.

How, then, in this theology, is the human person saved? What have the life, death and resurrection of Jesus to do with this inner loneliness? If Jesus was "like us in all things but sin," then he was free from the distrust of God that shows itself in discomfort with sexuality, anxiety over survival and dread of death. When we look at what we know of Jesus from the Gospels we find that his whole life centered around an experience of God that is uniquely familiar and intimate. This is expressed in Jesus' word for God, Abba. When Jesus announces the "reign of God" he speaks of the presence of a God who wants, and promotes, human well-being and happiness. Jesus lives free from anxiety over survival and invites his disciples to allow God to free them from anxiety. He openly enjoyed the company of women and treated them as equals. He moved toward his death freely and with trust.

The disciples were caught up in the Jesus movement. Men and women were invited into a close relationship with him and found themselves enormously attracted to him. What is the heart of this attraction? Sebastian Moore answers that while we normally know a God of desire who wants our happiness and also a God of control who instills a distrust of human happiness, Jesus knows and manifests only a positive view of God. In Jesus the disciples came to know the God who is Abba, the God who answers their own deepest desires. This must have been an exhilarating experience of freedom and joy.

Yet the disciples, caught up in this liberating experience of following Jesus, still had not dealt with the most challenging area of inner loneliness, death. The sheer intensity of their attraction to Jesus, the one free from sin, meant that failure and death became all the more lonely. Jesus had awakened desire in his companions, and he was the focus and the "containing symbol" of this desire. When Jesus was killed, the desire that had been awakened in his disciples comes to the point of radical crisis. Intensity of freedom and joy gives way to emptiness and total desolation.

The followers of Jesus entered into a world of emptiness and found the emptiness filled by the risen Jesus. They experienced Jesus alive beyond death. They found themselves empowered by the Spirit of God. Jesus now is the infinite One who answers the heart's loneliness. All of life is transformed in the encounter with the One who overcomes death. The disciples on Good Friday experienced a terrible death and found life beyond comprehension. They learned that in the whole of life there are experiences of helplessness and emptiness, and it is in these deaths above all that the power of the Spirit transforms us: "When I am weak, then I am strong."[30]

Jesus, the sinless one, aroused the desire for the end of inner loneliness in his disciples. In a unique way he opened up possibilities for freedom and intimacy with God. When Jesus, the awakener and the symbol of desire, is killed, then the disciples come to a point of irreversible crisis. Their meeting with the risen Lord means that the inner loneliness has met its resolution. The loneliness expressed in our sexuality, our earth dependence and our mortality is met by the One who has entered into death and overcome it. God is now revealed in Jesus Christ as the One who is our friend even in death, and as the One who brings us to life out of death.

5
Edward Schillebeeckx

Salvation is a central theme of Schillebeeckx's ongoing search for a contemporary Christology. In his book *Jesus: An Experiment in Christology* Schillebeeckx has already attempted to show how in Jesus of Nazareth we experience definitive salvation coming to us from God. His second major Christological work, *Christ: The Christian Experience in the Modern World*, deals explicitly with the theology of salvation and grace. This is a huge work of 925 pages, and here I will attempt only to outline the main systematic arguments of the book.

New Testament Theology

Schillebeeckx begins his book with a thorough discussion of human experience. He treats of the relationship between experiential encounters and the interpretation of these encounters in consciousness. One of his characteristic emphases is that the interpretative element in human experience is not to be seen only as something that occurs after an experiential encounter. He insists that an interpretative framework precedes a new experience. This interpretative framework, which is shaped by previous experiences, directs our perception of reality and opens up certain perspectives and not others. The element of interpretation is at the heart of human experience. Experience is always interpreted experience.[1]

A critical approach to experience will allow that our capacity for receiving new experience is conditioned by previous experiences, language, society and culture. Schillebeeckx argues that we grow in experience precisely when we come up against a reality that challenges our pre-conceptions and forces us to think again. When reality surprises us and proves to be different from what we expect, then what we experience clearly has objective validity. When new experience forces us to think again and calls into question our previous frameworks, then it has real authority. According to Schillebeeckx "the hermeneutical principle for the disclosure of reality is not the self-evident, but the scandal, the stumbling block of the refractoriness of reality."[2]

However Schillebeeckx does not want to oppose experience and tradition. Tradition is experience that has been shared, communicated and handed down to us. Whenever we have new experience, we experience it in the light of a tradition. It is tradition which makes understanding possible, but tradition also causes us to experience reality selectively. Schillebeeckx argues that traditions which can be open to the surprise of the new possess integrity, while traditions which cannot cope with new experience forfeit moral authority.

Revelation can be understood from this perspective. We come up against limits in our experiences and we know that reality is more than we can conceive or imagine. In these "boundary" experiences the question arises as to whether reality is not to be experienced as a gift, as grace. Are we addressed by reality in a personal way, by a personal God? This question arises in a tradition of religious language and religious faith. Schillebeeckx argues that experiences of God occur within ordinary human experience as "partial experiences" of meaning, or of salvation. Revelation occurs as the manifestation of transcendental meaning within our historical experience and in our "responsive affirmation'' of this manifestation. Revelation and the response of faith are two facets of the same reality. God is revealed as the ''inner reference'' of human life and human faith. God's action must not be reduced to the human response, but Schillebeeckx can say that ''only in historical human experience and human practice does revelation shine out as God's action.''[3] Revelation takes objective shape as the faith of the believing community. Revelation, however, must not be reduced to human interpretation. Rather it involves both ''the offer of revelation'' and the ''human, interpretative experience of revelation.''[4] It is not that one person, after an experience, interprets it as revelatory while another person does not. Rather the religious person truly *experiences* revelation and grace in the reality of life.

The New Testament is to be seen as the communication of God's revelation. In the New Testament the early Christian community, which had experienced salvation in Jesus, recognized the articulation of their faith experience. They recognized that the salvation they had experienced in Jesus had found authentic expression in the books of the New Testament. The Christian community, then, regards the Bible as a ''fragment of grace,'' a book which, like Jesus and his community, finds its inspiration in God.

The second and largest section of Schillebeeckx's book is concerned with the experience and interpretation of grace as it finds expression in the New Testament. Schillebeeckx begins with Paul, and then goes on to consider other New Testament authors, seeking to discover each author's view of salvation in Jesus.

Paul's theology is developed in the context of Jewish attempts to deal with the relationship between human conduct (as interpreted by the Torah) and being righteous in God's eyes. Schillebeeckx argues that in Jewish circles there was already the idea of justification by grace and the conviction that this grace finds its expression in the Torah. Paul does not simply contrast law and grace, or works and grace, but sets up the contrast between law as principle of salvation and Christ as principle of salvation.[5] Salvation does not come through the law (understood by Paul and his contemporaries as grace), but only through Jesus Christ.

Colossians is written in a very different context. Syncretic philosophies were threatening the Church community, offering *gnosis* (secret knowledge) and *pleroma* (divine fullness) through knowledge of cosmic beings, or heavenly angels. The response of Colossians is that in Christ alone we find the divine *pleroma*. In him the whole cosmos is created; he is the head of his body, the Church; in him all creation is reconciled by his death on the cross. Ephesians is written in a context where redemption myths were attempting to breach the wall between the world above and world below. It is written, as well, in full consciousness of the real divisions between nations, particularly the gap that separates Jew and Gentile. Ephesians argues that real unity and peace are based not on Roman rule, nor on redeemer myths, nor on the stoic *logos,* but on Christ: "He is our peace who has made us both one, and has broken down the dividing wall of hostility."[6] Ephesians argues that it is the Church's historical duty to manifest this peace of Christ to the nations.

In 1 Peter the question is: Why do the innocent suffer? In this context Jesus' expiatory suffering and death are presented as a model for suffering Christians. In imitation of Christ, Christian suffering can be an act of vulnerable love, benefiting even the oppressors by inviting them to change their ways.[7] Suffering is important in Hebrews too, but here Christian faith is presented to a group of people influenced by Jewish ideas and spirituality. Hebrews argues that temple worship is now superseded since in Jesus we have the One who, in self-sacrifice, gives himself in solidarity with his suffering brothers and sisters. Temple worship gives way to Christ, as in Paul law gives way to Christ.

John's Gospel is responding to a syncretic Moses-mysticism which is attractive to members of the Johannine community.

Moses, who has seen God face to face, is thought of as exalted with God and as mediating to initiates access to the vision of God. Against Sinaitic mysticism John's Gospel asserts that the access to God is through Jesus. Jesus, who comes from above, can bear witness to what he has seen and heard as pre-existent with God. He is the Word of God and to see him is to see the Father. Christian life (and salvation) consists in union with Jesus and with the Father, and in consequent love for one another.

For the Book of Revelation the context is set by the persecution of the Church by the state, particularly under Domitian. The Roman empire is seen as the servant of Satan, as the beast. The Lamb will triumph over evil and Christians will share in the victory of the Lamb, as the new Jerusalem. Jesus is presented as the one who assures final victory to a Church in conflict with historical evil in the form of a persecuting state.

In these summary paragraphs there is nothing of the richness of Schillebeeckx's exegetical treatment of New Testament authors (he has 125 pages on Johannine theology alone), but I have presented what I see as the most important outcome of his analysis. What emerges is that the one reality, salvation from God in Jesus, is experienced and interpreted differently in the various New Testament communities. Salvation is experienced and interpreted differently because of the different historical and cultural contexts of the various communities. They each have their own specific questions which they see answered in Jesus.

Schillebeeckx's close study of the various New Testament books provides a basis upon which he can offer a summary of, amongst other issues, the early community's understanding of grace, redemption and politics. The New Testament tells us that the grace of God comes to us in Jesus Christ in whom we find new possibilities for human living, and an invitation to live in communion with God. The climax of this is found in Jesus' love to the point of death, his resurrection and the bestowal of the Holy Spirit, the gift of salvation. The new way of life that is given in the grace of the Holy Spirit is called "adoption" by Paul and being "born from God" in John's theology.[8] The Christian, then, lives in communion with the Father, through the Son, in the Spirit. Schillebeeckx argues that this communion can be experienced, and that a Christian can make decisions about life on the basis of this experience.

As well as presenting us with this theology of grace, the New Testament speaks of our redemption, or liberation in Christ. Schillebeeckx examines the key concepts of the New Testament which describe this process: salvation and redemption; being freed from servitude and slavery; liberation through purchase or ransom; reconciliation after a dispute; satisfaction and peace; expiation of sins through a sin offering; the forgiveness of sins; justification and sanctification; salvation in Jesus as legal aid; being redeemed for community; being freed for love; being freed for freedom; renewal of persons and the world; life in fullness; victory over alienating and demonic powers.[9] Schillebeeckx shows how each concept is an analogy drawn from the experience and tradition of the people, and he discusses the biblical and historical background for each image.

He concludes this summary by arguing that the New Testament gives us specific details about the content of the freedom that Christians experience in Jesus. This is a freedom from specific oppressions and a freedom for a whole new life. It is freedom from such things as sin, guilt, the fear of demons, the anxiety connected with death, the anxiety about everyday matters, sorrow, despair, hopelessness, dissatisfaction with God and with other men and women, the lack of freedom, unrighteousness, oppressive and alienating ties, lovelessness, arbitrariness, egoism, credulity, the merciless condemnation of others, concern over one's reputation, panic, absence of pleasure and hopelessness.

It is freedom for such things as righteousness, peace between people and peace with God, confidence in life, new creation and the restoration of all things, joy and happiness, living and for life in eternal glory, love and hope, sanctification, ethical commitment, generosity and warmth, the sharing of goods and resources. In short, writes Schillebeeckx, we are "freed for salvation for the healing and making whole of each and every individual; to be 'imitators of God as beloved children' (Ephesians 5:1), 'to walk in love as Christ loved us' (Ephesians 5:2)."[10]

We are liberated from oppression and slavery in order to free others from injustice. We are redeemed within a "damaged and sick" world, and our salvation is "both a gift and a task to be realized." It is not an answer to simply divide salvation into objective and subjective dimensions. There is a real tension between the experience of liberation in Christ and the unhealed world to which we are directed. There is also a tension between what is given and what is done in our history and its eschatological fulfillment. Schillebeeckx puts it this way: "Everything has been *given* and everything is *to be done*."[11]

How does the New Testament apply this theology of salvation to social and political questions? One significant factor is that, in contrast to Greek thought, Jewish apocalyptic and Qumran, New Testament Christianity refuses to seek salvation in a world above. The two-level universe has been broken down since salvation has appeared in Jesus in the flesh. What Schillebeeckx calls the "critical variant" of Christianity is that we are called to live an ethical and religious life *in* the world, thanks to the forgiveness of sins.[12]

The early Christians felt called not only to attend to their personal conversions, but also to create a better human society on earth. However, there was no way they could influence the political structures of the Roman empire. Rather than retreat into another world the Christians opted to live out the life-style of the kingdom of God by creating new structures within their own community. They attempted the creation of a society in which no one lorded it over anyone else (Luke 22:25). 1 Peter indicates that they hoped that their own conduct and community life would form a challenge to the wider society. Schillebeeckx maintains that the demand for conversion still applies not only to persons but to structures. The New Testament option to focus on Church structures rather than the political structures of the wider community is a historically conditioned option. Today we must pursue the inner connection between grace and social consequences in new ways that meet the demands of our own times.

Is there any connection between the life of grace and political power in the New Testament? Schillebeeckx considers Romans 13 (where Paul pays great respect to civil authority), Revelation 13 (where the Roman empire is seen as a monster and the enemy of Christ) and Mark 12:13–37 (where Jesus is asked about paying taxes). He finds little that can be turned into dogmatic comment on the specific way Christians should approach politics. What he does argue is that while Jesus was not directly concerned with politics, his preaching and praxis of the reign of God (above all his way of dealing with the oppressed) have profound political implications and effects. The Gospels demand the kind of love for others that involves the transformation of those social and political structures which enslave people. On the other hand Schillebeeckx sees the absolutizing of political options as unbiblical: "Christianity knows nothing of the wrath which seeks to improve the world through inhumanity."[13]

Finally Schillebeeckx asks whether we are bound to continue to describe salvation in the way the New Testament does. It is clear that the New Testament uses various pre-existing "interpretative elements" to express the meaning of salvation in Jesus. Examples of such interpretative elements are the redemption of slaves, legal advocacy, and temple sacrifice. Schillebeeckx argues that we are not bound today to express our understanding of salvation in Jesus in terms of all of these interpretative images.[14] On the other hand we cannot simply select what we like from the Scriptures. Rather, Schillebeeckx argues, we must attempt to understand all the ways in which the New Testament expresses the experience of salvation and then we must find our own images which are capable of bringing joy and salvation to contemporary women and men. What we find in the New Testament is a variety of images and interpretative elements attempting to express the one saving action of God in Jesus; today we must be faithful to the New Testament by attempting to "inculturate" again the meaning of salvation and so keep our faith alive.

In the light of his study of the New Testament, Schillebeeckx suggests that there are four "structural elements" which must be taken into account in any attempt to reinterpret the Gospel message. The first of these has to do with God. God is the kind of God whose honor lies in human happiness and well-being. God has identified with us, above all with the poor, the exploited and the sinners, and in this God we find a totally positive answer to the question about the meaning of existence. This is a God whose heart is set on salvation. The second structural element in a theology of salvation has to do with Jesus. God's identification with us is finally disclosed in Jesus of Nazareth, in his message and manner of life, in his death and resurrection. Jesus is "God's countenance" turned toward us, the "nucleus" of God's history with women and men.[15] The third element is our own following of Jesus, as members of his community today—"by following Jesus, taking our bearings from him and allowing ourselves to be inspired by him, by sharing in his Abba experience and his selfless support for 'the least of my brethren' (Matthew 25:40), and thus entrusting our own destiny to God, we allow the history of Jesus, the living one, to continue in history as a piece of living Christology, the work of the Spirit among us, the Spirit of God and the Spirit of Christ."[16] The final element concerns the eschatological nature of definitive salvation—God's final salvation is not of this world or from this world. It remains beyond us, and yet in our earthly existence we do experience "fragments of salvation" which bear within themselves an inner promise of God's final salvation.

The Height and Breadth and Depth of Human Salvation

As Schillebeeckx begins to build a contemporary theology of salvation he approaches it from the perspective of human suffering. A theology of salvation for today must be a "critical remembrance of suffering humanity."[17] Schillebeeckx asks himself whether Christianity has something to say on this issue that can help us shape our history over the next thirty years. He believes that Christianity needs to offer a creative alternative to systems of thought like Marxism and "Critical Rationalism."

Both futuristic utopias (like Marxism) and conservative utopias (which attempt to recreate the past) tend to conceal within themselves the germ of movements hostile to humanity insofar as they absolutize one aspect of life. Marxism is rightly concerned about the cause of building a better world in the future, but when this cause becomes a divine absolute human life and dignity can become insignificant. On the other hand the "Critical Rationalism" of Karl Popper and Hans Albert leaves aside questions of meaning, and it seeks to build a better world through a pragmatic and scientific approach to life. It seeks to deal with the future through prognosis of future situations, rational forecasting of what can be brought about by deliberate action, and planning of action. The problem with this approach is that it has no way of dealing with major ethical questions, like our responsibility for ecology and the use of nuclear energy, since Critical Rationalism relegates questions of meaning to the private sphere. This means that in practice decisions are often made in the West (where Critical Rationalism is a dominant trend) on purely pragmatic and economic grounds.

Both Marxism and Critical Rationalism fail to allow that the future always escapes comprehension and transcends our human attempts at rational projection. Furthermore they fail to come to terms with important areas of human life. The most important of these is suffering. It is the critical remembrance of suffering humanity which challenges both utopian and pragmatic visions of life. Schillebeeckx raises the question of human suffering by a summary of the way major religions and systems of thought have dealt with it. He shows how all great religions are concerned with suffering, that they locate the cause of suffering in different places, and that therefore their actions to remove suffering differ. Marxism has perceived the causes of suffering to be economic and political and sought to act against suffering at this level. Schillebeeckx argues that suffering cannot be reduced only to personal and interior realities (the conservative religious position) nor to only economic problems (the Marxist position): "It is impossible to reduce the causes of suffering and the saving and redemptive action directed toward them *either* to merely personal *or* to exclusively socio-political action."[18] Schillebeeckx aims, then, at an understanding of humanity, human suffering and salvation, which can deal with such personal experiences as the confrontation with evil in one's life, and the facing of death, and which can deal also with economic and political realities. A realistic approach to suffering, and to salvation, will have to deal with all aspects of human existence in the world.

Two questions emerge when we confront human suffering. First, how are we to understand God's relationship to this world of suffering? Second, how are we to understand the human person, and human existence in the world? Schillebeeckx refuses to accept any easy rational explanations of suffering. He finds that after we have explained everything we can, there remains the "barbarous excess" of senseless suffering in our history.[19] How are we to relate this to our understanding of God?

Schillebeeckx rejects the view that God is the cause of both good and evil. He rejects the view of ancient Israel that the Lord is a God who "kills and restores to life."[20] He argues that Israel came to reject this primitive notion of God. For Schillebeeckx "God is pure positivity."[21] God does not want humankind to suffer. Schillebeeckx rejects as blasphemous the claim that God required the death of Jesus as compensation for our sins. Schillebeeckx offers no satisfying answers to the question of suffering. He regards it as incomprehensible. However he refuses to attribute it to God. In support of his position here he appeals to the theology of Thomas Aquinas. For Aquinas God is the first cause only of good. God created finite creatures and with finitude there is the possibility of a choice for evil. For Aquinas, and Schillebeeckx, negativity does not have its cause in God. From this Schillebeeckx will argue that there is no divine reason for the death of Jesus, and he can say that first of all "we are not redeemed *thanks* to the death of Jesus but *despite* it."[22] He admits that the expression that we are saved despite the death of Jesus does not say enough, and he has no intention of denying that God is the Lord of history who saves us through the death and resurrection of Jesus. However Schillebeeckx insists that God does not directly will the negative aspects of our history, including the death of Jesus. God is present in the death of Jesus precisely as overcoming evil and death itself. Negative aspects of history have an indirect role in God's plan in that God wills to overcome them. Belief in the resurrection means faith in God's victory over suffering and death and all negativity.

One of the most significant aspects of both Schillebeeckx's *Jesus* books is the unfailingly positive view of God that emerges in them. Throughout both books Schillebeeckx remains faithful to the centrality of the Abba experience for Jesus.[23] If Jesus' life and message centers on God as Abba, then a theology of redemption must also present God as boundless love. Schillebeeckx consistently presents a view of God as one who does not want humankind to suffer, who does not want (directly will) Jesus' suffering, but who through the death of Jesus is actively engaged in overcoming evil and suffering. There are difficulties with such an absolute stance on God as pure positivity, but Schillebeeckx prefers to live with the difficulties and the mystery rather than locate negativity in God.

If the view we have of God is absolutely crucial to a theology of salvation, so is the view we have of humanity. What is an adequate view of the human person? Schillebeeckx sees the focus of his own understanding of humanity in the concept of *"personal identity* within *social structure."*[24] He fills this concept out by arguing for seven "anthropological constants" which need to be always presupposed in any attempt to describe a livable human existence.[25] These anthropological constants do not give us specific norms or ethical imperatives, but rather general orientations and values which are valid in different historical situations. More specific norms for human living would need to be discussed from within a particular cultural context.

According to Schillebeeckx these seven constants need to be taken account of when discussing full humanity: (1) the relationship to human corporeality, nature and the ecological environment; (2) the relationship to other persons; (3) the connection with social and institutional structures; (4) the conditioning of people and culture by time and place; (5) the mutual relationship of theory and practice; (6) the religious and "para-religious" consciousness of the person; (7) the irreducible synthesis of these six dimensions. The last constant means that failure to recognize one of the six constants damages the whole.

According to Schillebeeckx salvation must be concerned with the whole system, with all the anthropological constants. He argues then that an adequate theology of salvation must connect the saving action of God with the body, with the ecological environment, with interpersonal relationships, with social and political structures, with the conditioning of people by time and place, with both theory and practice, and with the religious depths of the human person. A theology of salvation that deals only with ecology, or only with "being nice to one another," or only with the overthrow of an economic system, or only with mystical experience is inadequate and distorted.

Schillebeeckx discusses various theological attempts at relating "history" and "saving history."[26] He is clearly sympathetic to Metz's attempt to seek a political outline for the future from the Christian eschatological remembrance of Jesus Christ and from the critical remembrance of suffering humanity. He explicitly agrees with Kuitert that there is a "lowest limit" to salvation and this means that the concept of salvation must include as a minimum those social, institutional and political aspects necessary for human well-being. Schillebeeckx is also sympathetic to Gutierrez in his attempt to do theology from the point of view of enslaved and dependent humanity, in the centrality of praxis in his theology, and in the attempt to link redemption from sin and human liberation within a theology of liberation.

Schillebeeckx argues that earthly liberation must be considered as an inner component of Christian redemption, because the process of earthly liberation can be seen as a specific and necessary form of Christian love. Christian solidarity with human liberation is demanded by the Gospel. It has its own significance independently of whether it is the place for explicit evangelization. It has its own place as "minimum of salvation." However, any human liberation that claims to be a total liberation must be rejected as dangerous illusion; it ignores elements of human life and so reduces and impoverishes human beings. There is a salvation we need that we cannot supply ourselves. It can come only from God and "therefore the history of emancipation *cannot be identified* with the history of redemption from God, nor can the latter be detached from human liberation."[27] The attempt at human liberation which ignores the need for religious liberation ultimately becomes dangerous and alienating because it becomes blind to so much of human life.

What, then, is the connection between faith and politics? There are two principles to take into account. The first principle is the "eschatological proviso": a believer may not absolutize any political project, because the project cannot be identified with God or with God's eschatological salvation.[28] The second principle is that Christian revelation of God in Jesus directs us toward over-coming whatever enslaves humanity, and this includes all of what Schillebeeckx has called the anthropological constants. There is from the Gospel a "productive and critical impulse" which leads a Christian to act energetically for physical and psychological health, for freedom from humiliation, for freedom from oppressive and alienating social structures.

Christian faith contributes, then, both a critical impulse toward overcoming whatever enslaves people and the eschatological proviso which refuses to absolutize any movement to create a better world. It can contribute this critical foundation for political involvement only while it maintains its contemplative focus. Religious faith contributes to the world in and through its service to God. Only when Christians keep God at the center do they have a basis for criticizing what is dehumanizing without absolutizing any new social or political program.

Schillebeeckx asks himself whether the Gospel gives us any further direction for politics. He argues that analysis and interpretation must intervene between our understanding of the Gospels and our choice of a political party, and this analysis and interpretation must take account of many non-theological factors. There is no clear direction from the Gospels toward one political party. Schillebeeckx regards the following as being the appropriate Christian attitude to political action: "*On the one hand,* a politically relevant or politically active *church* or community of faith freely, without being tied to a political system or a political party, presents itself *qua* church as a critical consciousness of society and all its political parties from the point of view of both prophetic and ideological criticism; *on the other hand,* Christians combine with others who in common (fundamentally) share the same *political consensus,* in respect of a political program for the future.''[29] The Church must be a critical and prophetic voice, while it is up to the individual Christian to combine with others in political parties to seek justice and peace. Schillebeeckx suggests further that a two party system in a genuine democracy is a minimum political basis for a just society today. He also argues for a socialist political system, which is at the same time democratic and personalist.

God's Eschatological Salvation

If the believer can see salvation as partially realized in movements to create a free and just society, then this raises the question about final and complete salvation. When we look to the Gospels we find Jesus going about "doing good" and we discover salvation manifest, but manifest as a fragmentary anticipation of God's final salvation. Also, our experience of meaningless suffering has a "critical force" directing us toward God's future. We cannot, however, force the coming of final salvation and we cannot predict what depends upon God's freedom. We do know that God's glory lies in human happiness and we have been told that final salvation takes shape from what we do on earth (Matthew 25:34–40). However, the boundless mercy and goodness of God excludes the possibility that we can give a fixed content to God's salvation.

How is God's eschatological salvation connected with the death of Jesus? Schillebeeckx believes that it is disastrous to separate Jesus' death from his life: "The death of Jesus was no coincidence, but the intrinsic historical consequence of the radicalism of both his message and his life-style, which showed that all 'master-servant' relationships were incompatible with the kingdom of God."[30] The death of Jesus is the "historical expression of the *unconditional* character of his proclamation and practice."[31] Jesus so identified with the proclamation of a God concerned for humanity that the consequences became unimportant to him. Suffering and death for others is an expression of the radical and unconditional nature of a life lived for others. The resurrection shows forth the permanent validity of the death of Jesus and of the unconditional way of life that led to the death. It must be seen as an affirmation by God himself of this life and death, and of this unconditional identification with the suffering of others. ''God identifies himself with the person of Jesus, just as Jesus identified himself with God: God is love.''[32]

This death and resurrection assures Christians that suffering and death do not separate them from God. The negativity of death is vanquished since in Jesus God has transformed this negativity into life-giving communion. Christian hope in life after death is not a flight from the present. Rather it is the religious depth of the present that gives rise to the hope. Such hope should lead Christians to freedom and boldness before the power of evil. Resurrection faith thus becomes a powerful source of Christian action. The conviction about God's future for us should free us from anxiety and enable us to work more effectively in our world. Schillebeeckx calls this liberation from anxiety a ''piece of realized salvation.''[33]

The living God is our salvation. How is this saving God present to us? Schillebeeckx argues that God is present in ''mediated immediacy.'' On the one hand a human person has no unmediated relationship with God. God is mediated to us through history, through our world, through our neighbors and through ourselves. The experience of creation is the ''permanent breeding-ground'' for the experience of the saving nearness of God.[34] In Jesus we find God manifested in human form. God's saving grace is present to us not in some special area of inwardness but in the whole of life. Both inner freedom and social and political improvement form part of the grace of God.

On the other hand when we consider things from the divine side we can say that God is present to us in immediacy. The relationship with God is a unique one in which immediacy does not do away with mediation. Both aspects are necessary as we attempt to express the saving nearness of God. God is present in mediated form, yet in real immediacy, and the awareness of being grounded in God is the mystical power of faith. While salvation finds expression in all kinds of human liberation it is not identical with self-liberation. It is through the mystical aspect of faith that personal concerns and political concerns are transcended as God transforms from within. God's saving presence may be mediated through joyful experiences as well as negative experiences, or we may experience God as "dark night" when all our supports fall away. Prayer is the human attempt to attend to the nearness of God. Without prayer we tend to ground our lives in idols. Prayer, then, gives Christian life its most critical basis. [35]

Contemplation and transforming action are both essential aspects of Christian life. They are both connected through the unique epistemological power of suffering. Dissatisfaction with the continuation of the history of human suffering associates the contemplative with action for liberation. The Church must maintain the critical *memoria Christi,* showing by its action against suffering that it is a living remembrance of Jesus.

Schillebeeckx argues that salvation comes to us in and through our historical failures. While he disagrees with Moltmann's view that Jesus was abandoned by God on the cross, he believes that Jesus did experience the end of his life as a real failure, a "fiasco." [36] Jesus had to reconcile his failure with God and entrust his failure to God. The Gethsemane account tells us that Jesus did not completely understand his Father's way, and that he placed his trust in God despite the evidence of failure. The resurrection overturns this "failure" and overturns, as well, all human conceptions of success and failure. The experience of resurrection reveals that from God's side there was no failure. Jesus' failure acquires a productive and critical force in our history. It calls into question our historical successes and failures. Earthly success is not the way to full human healing. God identifies himself with one who takes upon himself such an historical fiasco as the cross, in love and faithfulness.

What does all of this have to do with salvation from sin?

Schillebeeckx sees a great difference between psychological and political liberation and liberation from sin and guilt. Only God can free us from sin, and the only answer for sin is: "He loved us while we were still sinners" (Romans 5:8). Justification through grace is therefore "the nucleus of salvation" in the light of which other aspects of liberation become comprehensible. The experience of God's love and forgiveness enables our human love to become the sacrament of God's love. Redemption is "being accepted by God" and it finds expression in our own "ortho-practic love."[37] Schillebeeckx agrees with Moltmann that "because reconciliation has come nearer in remembrance and hope, people begin to suffer because the world has not been redeemed."[38] The forgiveness of sins calls us to liberating action on behalf of others.

Redemption is never fully accomplished in our history, but we have the promise of definitive redemption in Jesus, and this final salvation is anticipated in our human acts of "doing good." These are "fragmentary" and "refractory" anticipations of definitive salvation which is not definable or grasped in itself. What we experience are anticipatory "fragments of salvation." However, "if the fundamental symbol of God is the living man (*imago Dei*), then the place where man is dishonored, violated and oppressed, both in his own heart and in a society which oppresses men, is at the same time the preferred place where *religious experience* becomes possible in a way of life which seeks to give form to this symbol, to heal it and give it its own liberated existence."[39] What matters is not the success of our actions—liberating, redemptive actions have meaning of themselves, and even in failure they open us up toward a new and greater future. Real redemption or salvation "always passes over into mysticism."[40]

Schillebeeckx has thrown great light on the question of the scope of salvation. His treatment of the "anthropological constants" has shown how salvation must relate to the body, to nature, to ecology, to interpersonal relationships, to social structures, to the conditioning of people by time and place, to the-

ory and practice and to our religious depths. He has shown the
connection between salvation and the excess of suffering in our
history. He shows how earthly liberation must be seen as an inner
component of Christian salvation. However, he also shows how
earthly projects of liberation cannot be identified with God's salvation. God's eschatological salvation always transcends what we
experience, and we cannot foresee or predict what depends upon
God's freedom. However, in our ordinary personal and social life
we do experience fragmentary anticipations of final salvation.
Schillebeeckx shows as well how the experience of failure in our
projects is transcended and overturned in the death and resurrection of Jesus. At the center of this theology of salvation is the experience of the forgiveness of sins. This is the "nucleus of
salvation"—and this experience of being accepted by God finds
expression in "orthopractic" love.

6
Liberation in Christ

In his letter to the Galatians Paul cries out: "For freedom Christ has set us free; stand fast, therefore, and do not submit again to a yoke of slavery" (5:1). Amongst other images for salvation, Paul sees Christ as the one who liberates us from sin, death and law (Galatians 2–5; Romans 6–8; 1 Corinthians 7–10). I find this concept of a threefold liberation a helpful model for a contemporary theology of salvation. As a way of addressing the questions raised in the opening chapter of this book, and as a way of responding to the theologies of Rahner, Gutierrez, Moore and Schillebeeckx, I will present my own reflections within this framework of a triple liberation.

Liberation from Sin, for Communion with God and Others:
Liberation from Collusion in Sinful Structures,
for Solidarity with the Poor and Action for Justice

As the exodus from Egypt led to the Sinai covenant, so the experience of salvation includes a liberation "from" and a freedom "for." At the most profoundly personal level salvation is liberation from sin and guilt, and freedom for intimacy with God. Each human person has the lonely and painful task of facing up to the fact that he or she has freely chosen to do evil. There comes a time when I can no longer place evil outside myself, but must face the reality that I have contributed to the store of the world's destructiveness and hatred. The most fundamental sense of sin comes when we are confronted explicitly with the boundless, unconditional love of God for us. In this experience we know not only our weakness and poverty but the fact that we are sinners. Acknowledgment of sin and guilt leads to humble prayer for forgiveness and the experience that this forgiveness is freely lavished upon us. The experience of forgiveness opens out into the possibility of a relationship of unspeakable nearness. The forgiven person is offered a relationship with the living God that answers the longings of the finite human heart for the infinite. The experience of forgiveness of sins and the kind of communion with God that John of the Cross describes in *The Spiritual Canticle* are both dimensions of our liberation in Christ Jesus.

Our sinfulness shows up, of course, in our destructive behavior toward others. Salvation begins to take hold in us when we recognize that we are indeed holding a grudge, or that we have labeled another person and denied his or her individual humanity, or when we have spitefully "put-down" another in order to feel better about ourselves. When God liberates us from sin in our inter-personal relationships the blinkers fall from our eyes and we see the true humanity of another. We know, in the movements of forgiveness, love, compassion and solidarity, the free gift of God's grace. This is the experience of salvation. God's salvation is experienced in our liberation from egoism, prejudice and hurt pride, and in our liberation for deeper affection, warmth and care, commitment and fidelity.

There is, moreover, a kind of evil that transcends any individual. It inhabits cultural traditions, economic systems, patterns of social relationship and political structures. Exploitation by transnational companies of badly paid workers in poor countries, the fact of starvation in a world rich in food, the arms race and the domination of women by men constitute "sinful situations" of enormous gravity in our world. There is no doubt that certain men and women can and do freely promote such evil systems. Sinful situations are caused to some extent by free people sinfully choosing what is evil. It is also true, however, that in many situations a sinful situation is maintained by people who do not consciously choose to do evil. There is a kind of collusion in evil that operates at an unconscious level when a group of people allow evil to happen, and perhaps benefit from it, without consciously facing up to what is happening. This collusion is undeniable in a century which has witnessed the atrocities of Nazi extermination camps.

In my own country Aboriginal people have had their land stolen, they have been decimated by introduced diseases, they have been forced into institutional living, they have been subject to racist laws and their culture has been largely eroded. White Australians live well, by and large, in a rich country. This good life exists because of the occupation of Aboriginal land. White Australians are part of a sinful destruction of Aboriginal life and culture. Of course there are many who are not racist, or personally guilty of exploitation, but they are still part of an exploitative and sinful situation.

How does salvation come to us in these kinds of situations? It seems to me that the recognition of being a participant in certain evil situations is the beginning of God's liberation. Once the situation is faced, then there is an absolutely crucial choice. We can retreat from the recognition and repress the growing awareness, and thus return to our collusion in evil. The alternative is a real movement toward solidarity with those who are the victims of the sinful situation. If I find myself, as an Australian, to be part of a white majority that has exploited and inflicted unimaginable misery on an Aboriginal minority, then the movement of salvation from God directs me toward solidarity with Aboriginal people. Liberation from sinful situations occurs in and through a movement of solidarity with the poor. This solidarity means real relationships, taking a public stand and taking sides on divisive issues. To be in solidarity with the marginalized is to make a choice to be in a "cognitive minority." This can be a painful liberation involving a significant change in life-style.

God's liberation is experienced in solidarity with the poor: in the gift that the poor have to give to those who join with them; in shared action which attempts to create more human structures and relationships; in celebration of the gifts of God and of life itself by those who work and struggle together. Liberation becomes a profoundly ecclesial event when members of the Christian community support each other in reflection on life, listening to the word of God and taking action in their lives. The community celebrates God's victory over sin and evil in the sacrament of reconciliation, and gathers to celebrate the Eucharist in solidarity with the poor, as an effective sign of the liberating presence of Jesus Christ in our world.

Liberation from Death and the Fear of Death: Liberation for a Free and Trusting Life

If it is true that our most fundamental fear is an all-pervasive anxiety about death, then the conviction that God liberates us in and through the darkness of death is central to a theology of salvation. This conviction springs from the disciples' encounter with the risen Lord. What had looked like total failure, and rejection by God, was proved to be something altogether different. God was at work in this historical failure and in this death, overcoming failure and death and bringing forth life in abundance. The resurrection experiences of the disciples provide the basis for the Christian belief that death, even though it seems like falling into an unknown abyss, is really a falling into the arms of God. Christian faith does not deny the difficulty and pain of death but understands its inner meaning as a coming home.

Not only our bodies, but also our projects collapse and die. The death and resurrection of Jesus assure us that God can and does give a future to our work. Our efforts to build a more human world are at best only a partial success, but if we are convinced that God can and does give the increase, then limited success, or failure, can be entrusted to God in the hope that in God's way and in God's time life will be given. The overcoming of death in the resurrection of Jesus does not provide us with only an assurance of personal survival with God. It opens up hope for a communal and global future. It also gives us the basis for viewing life with its successes and failures in a different way. If the future of our projects is entrusted to God, then we become free to work hard and faithfully even against the odds, knowing that what seems like failure can open out into God's future.

This means that there is a real liberation from anxiety that occurs amongst those who live their lives with faith in the resurrection. Not only the basic anxiety about death, but also our anxiety about the survival of our projects can be entrusted to God. Of course we Christians do not always allow ourselves to receive the liberation offered here, and we can be as anxious as anyone else. However when we do live in the power of resurrection faith, we find the freedom to work and to love without being obsessed by the outcome.

Connected with all of this is the question of our relationship to our bodies and to our sexuality. Liberation from the fear of death can also mean a new freedom to accept our frail and aging bodies. We are caught neither in a false spiritualism, which pretends the body is insignificant, nor in an obsessive preoccupation with health and youth and attractive appearance. There is a freedom, too, to live with the incompleteness of being male or female, since sexual identity is found ultimately in life with God. Everything does not have to be discovered and experienced within a few short years. Liberation which leads us to be more at home with our bodies, and our sexual incompleteness, also allows us to enter into a more creative relationship with the whole of nature. There is not the same need to exploit whatever can be had from the earth's resources in the next twenty years. Rather we can recognize that we are part of it all, part of the process of life and death, yet as conscious beings not ultimately terrified of death because of resurrection faith.

We experience God's salvation in the freedom we have to enjoy life to the full, to exult in the gifts all around us; yet we know there is no need to grasp at it or cling to it or try to possess it. Liberation from anxiety about holding onto possessions is at the heart of our experience of salvation:

Therefore I tell you, do not be anxious about your life, what you shall eat or what you shall drink, nor about your body, what you shall put on. Is not life more than food, and the body more than clothing? Look at the birds of the air; they neither sow nor reap nor gather into barns, and yet your heavenly Father feeds them. Are you not of more value than they? And which of you by being anxious can add one cubit to his span of life? And why are you anxious about clothing? Consider the lilies of the field, how they grow; they neither toil nor spin; yet I tell you, even Solomon in all his glory was not arrayed like one of these. But if God so clothes the grass of the field, which today is alive and tomorrow is thrown into the oven, will he not much more clothe you, O men of little faith?

Therefore do not be anxious, saying, "What shall we eat?" or "What shall we drink?" or "What shall we wear?" For the Gentiles seek all these things; and your heavenly Father knows that you need them all. But seek first his kingdom and his righteousness, and all these things shall be yours as well (Matthew 6:25–33).

Liberation from the Need To Justify Oneself: Liberation for Self-Acceptance and the Capacity for Vulnerable Love

Ernest Becker has pointed out that our fear of death is closely connected with the need to assert ourselves, to build ourselves up, to make something of ourselves. The assertion of self can be creative, but it can also be demonic when a person, a group, or a class can find meaning only by the domination of others.

The need to prove "I am somebody" manifests itself when I invest all my meaning in my success at the work I do, my home, my family, or my participation in a social or political cause. When I transfer onto a cause (whether the cause be my work, the success of my family, or disarmament) my need for significance, then the cause carries a weight it is unable to bear. A man or a woman who works hard for the sake of a family can discover, when success at work becomes loaded with proving oneself worthwhile, that work has dominated and destroyed family life and relationships.

Religious faith can be another form of self-assertion when individuals try to make themselves right before God by scrupulous attention to religious practices, or when they keep religious law rigorously in order to justify themselves before God. The "holier-than-thou" caricature of the religious person has its origin in the fact that religious faith can easily become another arena in which a person builds up the sense of self by putting others down.

The Gospels present us with the radically different stance of Jesus. Jesus of Nazareth engaged in a struggle against the view that we can earn our way into God's favor, that there are religious "insiders" and "outsiders." He presented an image of the reign of God in which, incredibly, those who had done little work were paid at the end of the day at the same rate as those who had worked all day (Matthew 20:1–16). He presented a picture of God as preoccupied with the "lost," with the outsiders (Luke 15). God, for Jesus, is One who gives freely and bountifully to all who approach in need.

Paul carries on this tradition in his theological position that through the cross of Jesus we are liberated from law. At this point I want to leave aside the historical question to what extent the contemporaries of Jesus and of Paul were caught up in a religion of self-justification. I think it likely that they were not more trapped by a focus on self than devout religious men and women of other ages. The important issue is the fact that self-justification remains a danger for all religious faith. It can become simply another attempt at proving oneself significant by performing so well that one stands out from the crowd. What Paul says to all of this is that we are not saved by our own performance, even by performance of the holy law of God. We are saved by the sheer grace of God poured out in our world in and through Jesus Christ. We are saved "in Christ," and "in Christ" we are liberated from the human need of proving ourselves significant.

Through being taken into Christ I am significant and worthwhile. Significance comes not from what I do nor from how others perceive me but from the stunning fact that God judges me not only worthwhile but lovable with an infinite love. The experience that I am beloved of God is a most profound liberation from the need to justify myself.

For Paul the crucified Jesus is the permanent sign that justification comes not from our own efforts but from the free gift of God (Galatians 3:1). We are liberated from the need to prove ourselves right because "God's love has been poured out into our hearts through the Holy Spirit which has been given to us" (Romans 5:5). This experience of liberation provides freedom and space in life.

Insofar as my work and my projects are freed from the loading that comes when they carry the need to prove myself, then I am liberated to work in freedom and peace. In the death and resurrection of Jesus there is freedom from the need to possess, because it is not possession that gives meaning. I can accept and love myself because I am loved by the God of Jesus. This frees others from my tendency to expect them to be God for me. I am less likely to expect others to meet my boundless needs. There is freedom to take risks, to make space for others, to forgive and to love.

The Cross and Human Salvation

Along with the four theologians considered in this book I believe that the popular image of redemption, as propitiation of God's anger by the sacrificial death of Jesus, is distorted. A view of redemption in which God is pacified by suffering and death does not do justice to God. Most of us would think of a human person who insisted on propitiation for an offense through suffering as sadistic. Yet we have attributed this kind of attitude to God. In doing so we have been unfaithful to Jesus' view of God.

I believe it is evident that the heart of Jesus' preaching and practice has to do with God and God's rule. In Jesus' ministry of healing and forgiveness, in his parables of the reign of God, in his association with outcasts and sinners, and in his prayer, we find a view of God as the One who is always turned toward us offering unconditional love and limitless mercy. If we construct a theology of redemption that undermines this understanding of God, then there is something wrong with our theology of redemption.

If the redemption is not about pacifying God, or about changing God's mind, how are we to understand the death of Jesus? What connection is there between Jesus' death and our salvation? Is there still some real sense in which Jesus died ''for us,'' so that we can say that his death is the cause of our salvation?

It seems to me that there are two important points to be made here. The first is that the death of Jesus must not be isolated either from his life, on the one hand, or from his resurrection, on the other hand. First, then, Jesus' death must be seen as the consequence of the radical nature of his life and message. His passionate stance for the rule of God meant both the glad tidings that God loves us with an abandon we cannot imagine, and the consequent challenge that all relationships and structures built upon dominance and exploitation are unfaithful to this God who gives priority to the marginalized and the sinner. The death of Jesus is the outcome of a life lived in fidelity to this view of God. Jesus' preaching and liberating practice unsettled others, and had disturbing consequences for both religious life and political institutions. Amidst growing opposition on all sides Jesus remained faithful to his experience of a saving God, even when this meant facing death at the hands of the Romans.

Jesus' proclamation of the reign of God was a proclamation that God's salvation was already taking effect in his own ministry. The liberation had begun. Even in the failure of his movement, and in his death, Jesus remained faithful to God, and was able to trust still that God is the One who saves. The resurrection experience empowered the disciples to see that God's salvation was not defeated by death, but accomplished in spite of apparent failure, and in spite of death. It was being accomplished in and through the whole life of Jesus, right up to and including his death. His death, his final entrusting of everything to God, is now seen as the culmination of Jesus' life. On reflection, and in the light of resurrection, the Church could see that the death of Jesus was our liberation from death. "Sin," "death" and "law" are overcome in Jesus' victory over death. The good news that Jesus proclaimed, God's salvation, is made manifest in his death and resurrection in the most radical way possible.

Even death, the final obstacle, is transformed by God's saving hand. In the resurrection experience Jesus stands revealed as not just the one who proclaims our freedom, but as himself Savior and Liberator. When Jesus' death is seen as the outcome of his liberating stance in life, and when the resurrection is seen as God bringing salvation even in this death, then we get a glimpse of what it means to say we are saved by the death of Jesus.

The second thing to be said in this context is that Karl Rahner offers us a viable way of understanding how we can hold together the view that God is present to each person as a permanent offer of salvation, with the traditional doctrine that the cross of Jesus is the cause of our salvation. In a sacrament the sacramental symbol expresses God's grace and is also the cause of grace. In a similar way the death of Jesus is the cause of salvation in the sense that God's universal will to save finds its definitive and effective expression in the life, death and resurrection of Jesus. The cross is the real symbol of salvation, and as a real and effective symbol it is the cause of the saving grace offered to each person.

The Experience of Salvation Today

Do we actually experience salvation? I believe that we must answer yes to this question. Of course, the claim that salvation is experiential is not a denial that salvation is first of all God's saving will, taking effect through the power of the Holy Spirit, and made definitively manifest in the life, death and resurrection of Jesus. Salvation is not something that can be reduced to our human consciousness. But it is something that can take hold in our lives through human experience. It occurs as a yes, either explicit or implicit, to the mystery of grace at the heart of life. It comes upon us as an experience that we are forgiven and loved beyond measure. It occurs at the heart of relationships with others, in moments of reconciliation, in the experience of community, in participation in action that seeks justice and peace. It occurs also in the silence of prayer and in gathering with others to break bread in memory of Jesus.

At the beginning of this study I discussed four issues that confront us with extraordinary urgency as we approach the year 2000: the real possibility of total nuclear destruction, the economic exploitation and misery of so much of the earth's population, the ecological crisis and the emerging awareness of the way women are dominated by men. These realities loom before us as complex and overwhelming. Yet it seems clear that they are the places where we are called to conversion today. A contemporary theology of salvation must offer us hope as we face the issues of peace, economic justice, the environment and sexual equality. Christian faith affirms that "where sin increased, grace abounded all the more" (Romans 5:20), and I believe this is as true of structural evil as it is of personal sin. These massive problems can be seen to be, in the light of Christian faith, the place where God offers us liberating grace. Wherever we freely confront these issues and open our hearts to conversion in and through them, then they become the place of salvation.

In fact when we look at what is happening in our world we can find reasons for hope. There is a growing peace movement all around the world uniting millions of people on our globe. There are people working together for new political and economic structures at the level of small grass-roots groups and at the level of national and international politics. The movement toward responsible care for our environment is just beginning to have a real political impact. Women are becoming aware of the fact of their domination and have begun what I believe is an irreversible movement toward equality. Each of these movements unites people who hold various political and religious opinions, but Christians can rejoice that there is also a Christian presence in each movement. We can look too at such hopeful signs as the emergence of basic Christian communities, the prophetic witness of people like Dorothy Day and Helder Camara, the Christian peace groups, the work of female and male theologians, and the recent statement on peace and disarmament by the bishops of the United States of America. There are many other movements of conversion and hope, and there are millions of Christians who work actively with others for political and social change in groups which are not specifically Christian.

The question is: May we see these hopeful movements of

conversion and hope, whether they be explicitly Christian or not, as the place where God is acting today to save and liberate? The answer to this can only be yes. However, there is need for a qualification that is essential. God's final liberation remains beyond our grasp and we do not control God or God's future salvation. I cannot identify my project and my group with God's salvation. I have to recognize that my project is subject to distortion from human weakness and sinfulness. However, I can still see in it the signs of God's saving grace already present and active. In all kinds of experiences within the movement of change I can know that "all is grace": in the moment when a person truly confronts evil, in the experience of solidarity with others, in self-forgetful love, in compassion for the enemy, in common action, in the joy of good achieved and in the endurance of failure.

The movements toward peace, justice, ecological responsibility and sexual equality are places where God's salvation is present and operative, as foretaste and promise of God's final salvation. They are a real experience of salvation breaking in upon life. However they remain human and provisional and subject to sin. They can never be absolutized, but always remain open to criticism and challenge. There remains the need for the discernment of spirits. For a Christian the critical base for this discernment is the experience of the living God who transcends all our projects. Above all there is the critical force of the Gospel with its view of the God whose love is humankind and whose priority is for those who are marginalized.

Notes

Chapter 1
Salvation at the End of the Twentieth Century

1. Paul uses the word *hilastērion,* an apparent reference to the mercy seat set upon the ark in the Holy of Holies, used on the Day of Atonement (Exodus 25:17–22; Leviticus 16:14).

2. *Adversus haereses* 5.17.3.

3. *Ibid.,* 3.18.1.

4. Irenaeus writes: "He was made an infant for infants, sanctifying infancy, a child among children, sanctifying this age . . . " (*Adversus Haereses* 2.22.4).

5. *Ibid.*

6. *De incarnatione* 54:3.

7. J.P. Kenny writes: "For him 'to adopt as a son' (*Huiopoiein*) and 'to deify' (*Theopoiein*) are interchangeable expressions" ("Divinization in the Greek Fathers of the Church," *Compass* 18, 1984, page 25).

8. *Orationes contra Arianos* 2.67.

9. See, for example, John of the Cross in *The Spiritual Canticle* 39, 5–6.

10. In *Cur Deus Homo?* Anselm writes: "None can make this satisfaction except God. And none ought to make it except man . . . " (2:6). See also Chapter 6 of *Cur Deus Homo?*

11. See Anselm's comment: "But God cannot properly leave any-

thing uncorrected in his kingdom. To remit sin without punishment would be treating the sinful and the sinless alike, and this would be incongruous to God's nature, and in incongruity is injustice" (*Cur Deus Homo?* 1.12).

Chapter 2
Karl Rahner

1. For a summary of Rahner's position see his *Foundations of Christian Faith* (New York: Seabury Press, 1978). The foundations for Rahner's thought can be found in his metaphysics of knowledge—*Spirit in the World* (New York: Herder and Herder, 1968)—and his philosophy of religion—*Hearers of the Word* (New York: Herder and Herder, 1969).

2. Rahner argues that God makes himself a "constitutive principle of the created existent without thereby losing his absolute, ontological independence" (*Foundations*, page 120). He is here invoking his theology of "formal causality," arguing that God, by grace, becomes a constitutive element in a human person through self-communication.

3. *Foundations*, page 116.

4. "Concerning the Relationship Between Nature and Grace," *Theological Investigations* 1:297–317.

5. "Nature," then, for Rahner is a "remainder concept" (*Restbegriff*). See "Concerning the Relationship Between Nature and Grace," page 313.

6. *Foundations*, page 143.

7. *Ibid.*

8. On this question see "Christianity and the Non-Christian Religions," *T.I.*, 5:115–134; "Anonymous Christians," *T.I.*, 6:390–398; "Atheism and Implicit Christianity," *T.I.*, 9:145–164; "Anonymous Christianity and the Missionary Task of the Church," *T.I.*, 12:161–178; "Observations on the Problem of the 'Anonymous Christian,' " *T.I.*, 14:280–294; "Anonymous and Explicit Faith," *T.I.*, 16:52–59; "The One Christ and the Universality of Salvation," *T.I.*, 16:199–224; "On the Importance of the Non-Christian Religions for Salvation," *T.I.*, 18:288–295.

9. Rahner is not wedded to the term. See his remarks in "Obser-

vations on the Problem of the 'Anonymous Christian,' " page 291 and page 292.

10. *Lumen Gentium,* 16; *Gaudium et Spes,* 22; *Ad Gentes,* 7; *Nostra Aetate,* 1.

11. "Christianity and the Non-Christian Religions," *T.I.* 5:125.

12. "The One Christ and the Universality of Salvation," *T.I.* 16:206–207.

13. *Ibid.,* page 207.

14. *Foundations of Christian Faith,* page 255.

15. "The One Christ and the Universality of Salvation," page 211.

16. *Ibid.,* page 212.

17. *Foundations of Christian Faith,* page 284.

18. Jesus Christ, is, then, the *"Ursakrament."* See "The One Christ . . . " page 215.

19. "The One Christ and the Universality of Salvation," page 221.

20. *Foundations of Christian Faith,* page 295.

21. *Ibid.,* page 296.

22. *Ibid.,* page 297.

23. Rahner sometimes uses the word "memory" to describe the anticipation of the absolute Savior: "Jesus Christ is always and everywhere present in justifying faith because this faith is always and everywhere the searching memory of the absolute saviour" (*Foundations,* page 318).

Chapter 3
Gustavo Gutierrez

1. The first chapter in his *A Theology of Liberation* (Orbis: Maryknoll, New York, 1973) is concerned with methodology. His more developed thinking can be found in *The Power of the Poor in History* (SCM: London, 1983), particularly in part IV, pages 169–234.

2. *A Theology of Liberation,* page 11; *The Power of the Poor in History,* page 103.

3. *A Theology of Liberation,* pages 13–15.

4. *Ibid.,* page 11.

5. *The Power of the Poor in History,* pages 90–106, 212.

6. *Ibid.*, pages 171–185.
7. *Ibid.*, pages 185–214.
8. *Ibid.*, pages 92, 193, 213.
9. *Ibid.*, page 207.
10. *Ibid.*, pages 203, 231. See Dietrich Bonhoeffer, *Letters and Papers from Prison*, new greatly enlarged edition (New York: Macmillan, 1972), page 17.
11. *The Power of the Poor in History*, page 102.
12. *Ibid.*, page 103.
13. See his remarks in the interview "Latin American's Pain Is Bearing Fruit" in *A New Way of Being Church* (Lima: Latin America Press, 1984), page 3.
14. *A Theology of Liberation*, pages 53–72.
15. This is a significant part of Gutierrez's argument which I am not able to reproduce adequately in this space. It is important to recognize this reality because Gutierrez is not arguing in the abstract, but, as I have already pointed out, doing theology as a "second act," as a reflection on the process of liberation. See his outline of the historical context in *A Theology of Liberation*, pages 81–131.
16. *A Theology of Liberation*, page 153.
17. *Ibid.*
18. *Ibid.*, page 159.
19. *Ibid.*, page 167.
20. *Ibid.*, page 174.
21. *Ibid.*, page 175.
22. This distinction is made early in *A Theology of Liberation*, pages 36–37. See also pages 176–178.
23. *A Theology of Liberation*, page 177.
24. *Ibid.*
25. *Ibid.*
26. *We Drink from Our Own Wells* (Maryknoll, New York: Orbis, 1984), page 99.
27. *Ibid.*, page 111.
28. *Ibid.*, page 112.
29. *Ibid.*, page 117.
30. *Ibid.*, page 119.
31. *Ibid.*, page 127.

32. *Ibid.*, page 132.
33. *Ibid.*, page 135.

Chapter 4
Sebastian Moore

1. *The Crucified Is No Stranger* (London: Darton, Longman and Todd, 1977), *The Fire and the Rose Are One* (London: Darton, Longman and Todd, 1980) and *The Inner Loneliness* (London: Darton, Longman and Todd, 1982). Moore's *Let This Mind Be in You* (London: Darton, Longman and Todd, 1985) arrived after the manuscript of this book was completed.
2. *The Denial of Death* (New York: The Free Press, 1973).
3. *Ibid.*, page 51.
4. *Ibid.*, page 53.
5. *The Crucified Is No Stranger,* page 14.
6. *Ibid.*, page 19.
7. *Ibid.*, page 21.
8. *Ibid.*, page 23.
9. *Ibid.*, page 57.
10. *Ibid.*, page 58.
11. These remarks are made in the summary introduction to the book, page xii.
12. *The Crucified Is No Stranger,* page 91.
13. *The Fire and the Rose Are One*, page xi.
14. *Ibid.*, page 11.
15. In fact Moore speaks of a "natural" love affair with God (pages 22–27). It seems clear that this is already a gift of grace and what Rahner calls the supernatural existential.
16. *Ibid.*, page 67.
17. *Ibid.*, page 71.
18. *Ibid.*, page 83. On the same page Sebastian Moore writes that "the sense of the sheer vitality of God can burst upon the soul and be named Holy Spirit."
19. *Ibid.*, page 145.
20. In the introduction to his next book (*The Inner Loneliness*)

Moore acknowledges his debt to Jon Sobrino's *Christology at the Cross-roads* as a source for his approach to the disciples' experience. For Moore's reservations about his earlier work see the three chapters of "retractions" in *The Fire and the Rose Are One*, pages 129–147.

21. *The Inner Loneliness* (London: Darton, Longman and Todd, 1982).

22. *Ibid.*, page 18.

23. *Ibid.*, page 22.

24. *Ibid.*, page 25.

25. *Ibid.*, page 28.

26. *Ibid.*, page 38.

27. *Ibid.*, page 49.

28. Moore takes his construct of the three ages from Karl Jasper's understanding of the "axial shift" that occurred in human consciousness two and a half thousand years ago. Moore (page 54) sees the tragedy *Oedipus Rex* as a cultural response to the first great axial shift.

29. *The Inner Loneliness*, page 68.

30. *Ibid.*, page 91.

Chapter 5
Edward Schillebeeckx

1. *Christ: The Christian Experience In the Modern World* (London: SCM, 1980), page 31.

2. *Ibid.*, page 35.

3. *Ibid.*, page 48.

4. *Ibid.*, page 50.

5. *Ibid.*, page 126.

6. Ephesians 2:14.

7. Thus 1 Peter 3:16 reads: "And keep your conscience clear, so that, when you are abused, those who revile your good behavior in Christ may be put to shame." Schillebeeckx remarks: "Putting to shame those who revile good behavior is a matter of the innocent victim making his tormentor think and perhaps converting him" (*Christ*, page 227).

8. *Christ*, page 464.

9. Schillebeeckx analyzes sixteen key concepts from the New

Testament which express the significance of redemption in an extremely useful way on pages 477–511 of *Christ*.

10. *Christ*, page 513.

11. *Ibid.*, page 514.

12. "From now on man can live a moral and religious life *in* the world, thanks to the forgiveness of sins, and that means—in terms of the world-view of time—living a 'heavenly' life, but on earth. In other words, from now on some of the kingdom of God can be realized *on earth*" (*Christ*, page 558). Schillebeeckx calls this the "exodus character" of Christian life.

13. *Christ*, page 586.

14. In his *Interim Report on the Books Jesus and Christ* (London: SCM, 1980), Schillebeeckx remarks: "Pictures and interpretations which were once appropriate and evocative can become irrelevant in another culture. Or within our present culture, which regards, for example, the ritual slaughter of animals as repulsive, it is highly questionable whether we should go on describing the saving significance of the death of Jesus as a bloody sacrifice made to an angry God who needed it in order to be placated. In modern conditions this is likely to discredit authentic belief in the real saving significance of the death: it goes against all critical and responsible modern experiences" (page 16).

15. *Christ*, page 639.

16. *Ibid.*, page 641.

17. *Ibid.*, page 670.

18. *Ibid.*, page 716.

19. *Ibid.*, page 725.

20. 1 Samuel 2:6.

21. *Christ*, page 727.

22. *Ibid.*, page 729.

23. In *Jesus: An Experiment in Christology* (New York: Seabury, 1979) a very important section of the book has the heading "Jesus' Original *Abba* Experience, Source and Secret of His Being, Message and Manner of Life" (page 256).

24. *Christ*, page 734.

25. *Ibid.*, pages 734–743.

26. *Ibid.*, pages 746–762.

27. *Ibid.*, page 769.
28. *Ibid.*, pages 773–779.
29. *Ibid.*, page 784.
30. *Ibid.*, page 794.
31. *Ibid.*, page 795.
32. *Ibid.*, page 796.
33. *Ibid.*, page 801. In *God Among Us: The Gospel Proclaimed* (London: SCM, 1983) Schillebeeckx writes: "Eternal life is future which has already begun. If it has not already begun in our love and care for our fellow men, then eternal life is an ideology and an illusion, a phantom" (page 142).
34. *Christ*, pages 810–811.
35. Schillebeeckx writes: "Therefore prayer—and I think only prayer—gives Christian faith its most critical and productive force" (*Christ*, page 817).
36. *Christ*, page 823.
37. *Ibid.*, page 834.
38. *Ibid.*
39. *Ibid.*, page 837.
40. *Ibid.*, page 838.